PHOTOPC OF STAFFORDSHIRE

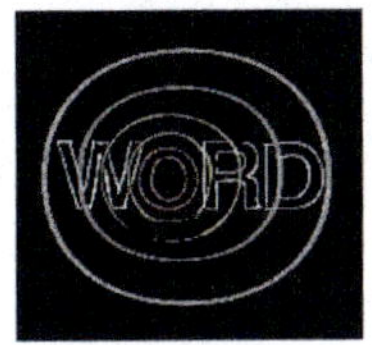

A photopoetry collection by WORD Stafford

in support of Katharine House Hospice

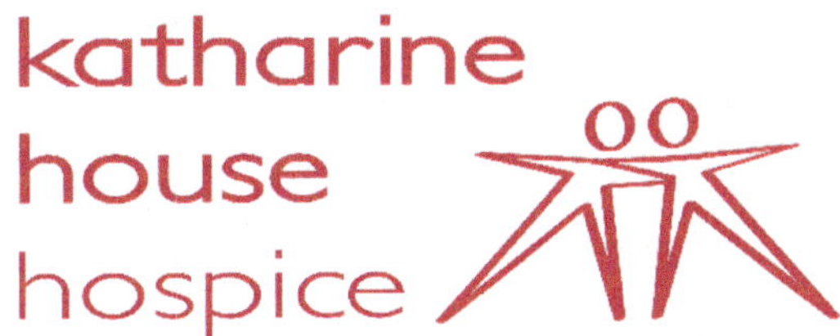

Various Authors

Edited by Mel Wardle Woodend

Cover Art by A Blind Photographer

PHOTOPOEMS OF STAFFORDSHIRE

First Printing: 2022

ISBN: 978-1-7399337-8-4 (DREAM WELL WRITING LTD)

DREAM WELL WRITING LTD

UNITED KINGDOM

www.dreamwellwriting.simplesite.com

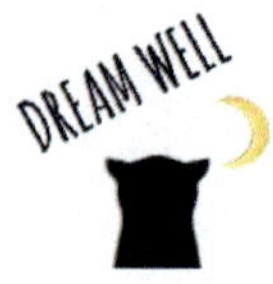

A Dyslexia Friendly Publication

DEDICATION

This book is dedicated to the memory of Mal Dewhirst – the first Poet Laureate of Staffordshire.

CONTENTS

FOREWORD

Staffordshire

In the heart of the country locked by land,
we may not have a coastline but we are grand.
Hills and moorlands, there are lots of beauty spots,
Although Stoke and Lichfield are the only cities we have got!

Alton Towers and the Staffordshire Hoard,
Staffordshire Bull Terriers, you won't get bored.
The murderous history of the Staffordshire knot,
three criminals put to death, so our county will not be forgot.

Railways and canals, lots of castles too.
You can never get bored there's so much to do!

Billy Fishwick

ACKNOWLEDGEMENTS

Thanks are due to each of the contributors to this anthology, for taking the time to take a photograph and write an inspired poem, with a Staffordshire theme.

Your thoughtful and creative contributions have made it possible for this anthology to be published in order to raise money for Katharine House Hospice in Stafford.

INTRODUCTION

Katharine House Hospice is a well known and incredibly important charitable organisation, based in Stafford. Not only do they provide care and support to their patients – but to the patients' families and loved ones. At WORD Stafford we feel Katharine House Hospice does extraordinary work and we wanted to find a way to support this local charity, as they support so many people in our local community.

We set a challenge by asking for submissions of photographs and accompanying poems (or maybe poems with accompanying photographs) – whichever inspired the other. The one specification we set was that these had to, in some way, have a Staffordshire theme.

Narrowing down the submissions to decide which to include is always a hard task – and we found the standard of entries submitted to this project were very high, however, we hope you will agree that the photopoetry sets selected provide a wonderful variety of insights into the Animals and Nature, and the People and Places of Staffordshire. All profits from the sales of this book (after print costs) will be donated to Katharine House Hospice.

Mel Wardle Woodend
Staffordshire Poet Laureate 2019-2022
and Director of Dream Well Writing Ltd

PART ONE

ANIMALS AND NATURE

Apothecary Garden

Inspired by the Erasmus Darwin Physic Garden

In Memory of ML

Come through the open
green door. There is thyme in this
garden- balm, healing
rosemary. Lavender to
calm. Poppies, inducing sleep.

Pink hyssop for coughs,
cornflowers cleansing tired eyes,
borage for colic,
marigold and vetiver
for nourishing aging skin.

Valerian for
anxiety. Infusing
chamomile, or green
nettle tea. Syrupy rose
of cinnamon-scarlet hips.

Blessed thistle to
coax appetite. For aching
heads - lady's slipper,
sweetest clove. Angelica,
cooling and white. Ginger for

nausea, fighting
disease. Sage for Memory.
Burdock - soothing throats,
yarrow for stimulation-

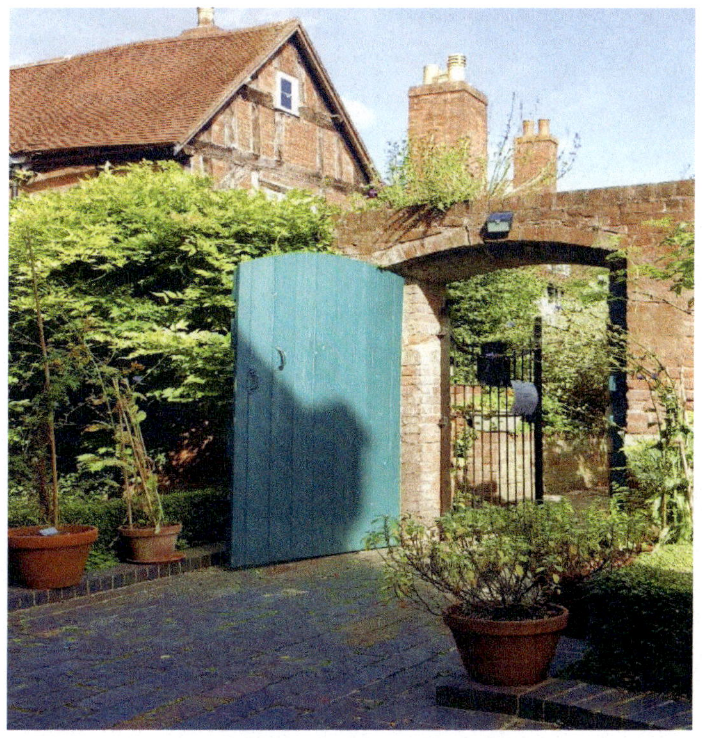

Physic garden of delight.

Susan Wood

Dead Water

Water, has its own modus operandi.
It doesn't shout until it destroys.
It listens to whispered secrets
of those passing by or discordant singing
of noisy revellers drunk on freedom.

It glides by riverbanks
and gardens, where on a November
morning names carved
on cold stone memorials hang
like a lament.

It does not regret loss.
It is deaf to the choking
sound of a parent's pain or melancholy
calls of gulls hovering.

Each disturbance is no more
than the tattooing of rain,
or the gliding of wildfowl
on its surface.

Water is an old machine,
sometimes noisy, often smelly.
If neglected, it dies.

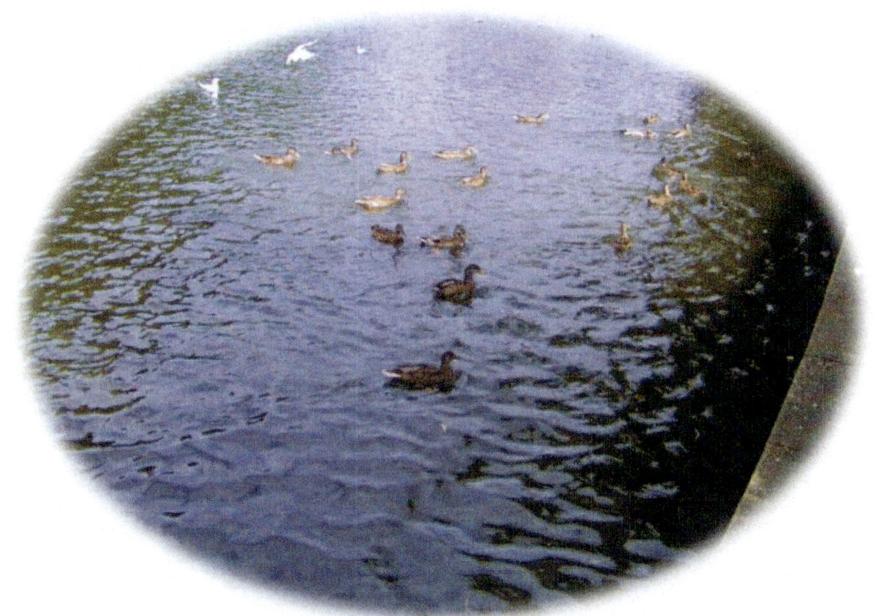

Wildfowl on Minster Pool, Lichfield

Marjorie Neilson

Freezing Fog

Down in the valley, along the stream, lies the freezing fog

tendrils of mist hanging over the water, over the grass, curling sinuously

it creeps up the banks, over the field, through the park, enveloping the copse -

a ghostly mist leaving solid footprints:

a world encased in rime

haunting beauty, a chilly desolation

coating everything in sparkling crystal glass

frozen - locked - in a moment

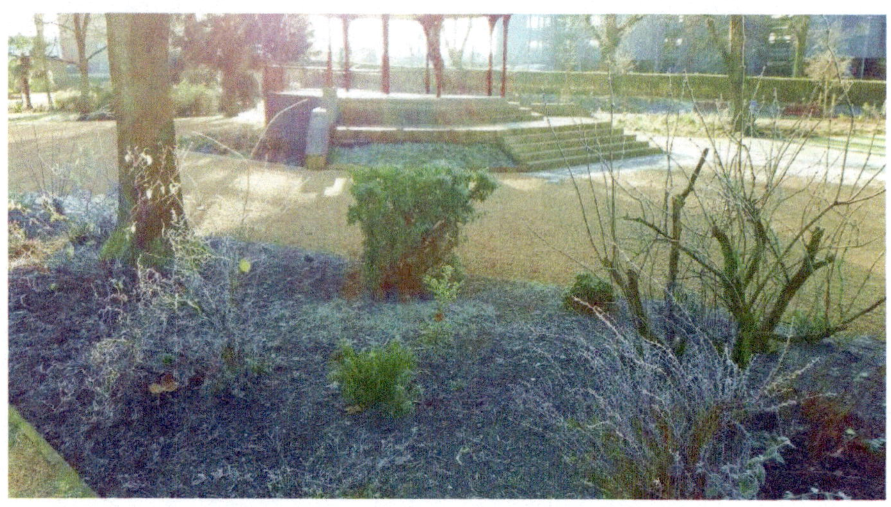

Rime Frost in Victoria Park, Stafford

Tom Lawrence

Goatsuckers

Caprimulgus europaeus: the nightjar

Cannock Chase, Staffordshire

This haunting lowland heath, as cauling dark
distils from light; breathless, I'm scarecrow-still.
How student friends would laugh. One moment it's
the hobby, home from slicing through dense clouds
of swifts, like tickertape, on marshes by
the Sow, next trawling swallow morphs to bat.
Day folded into night, one blink, the stir
of insect armies changing shift, time stalls.
They chirr, invisible till dervishes
angling for moths or teats of goat appear,
enchanted by a Samuel Palmer sky.
One lands, a tipsy high-rise ace of spades
or tightrope walker feigning life and limb
as cuckoos do, the audience spellbound.

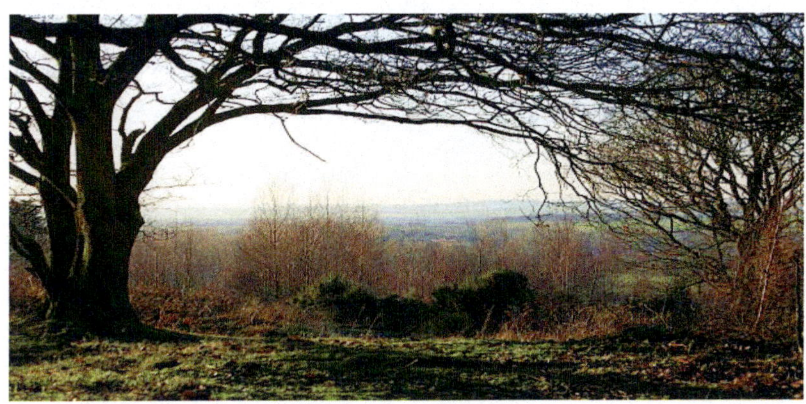

Cannock Chase

Peter Branson

Lost between Abnalls Lane and Cross in Hand
OS Pathfinder 872, 892

No waste in seamless piecing of meadow, stream, copse –
nature man made, hewn, hacked by hard hands;
clay, stones, water, all sweat stained, salted,
seasoned by shed blood, ground bone.

Intricate sound stitching; gilt thread larksong
weaving into Ashbrook's chatter, pines creaking
loud as uprising wind rush under kestrel's wings,
sky lover skrying lordly over his larder.

Secrets in hedges' tight, dark hearts –
hidden lives beating muffled by branches
interlaced, lichen crusted, thorn guarded,
new nettles quickening, bramble's tripping wire.

Bewildered, led astray in folded fields by twisting views,
trees' conspiracies mystifying map's directions;
narrow acres become infinite fractal space –
worlds wheel, spinning in blackbird's gold ringed eye.

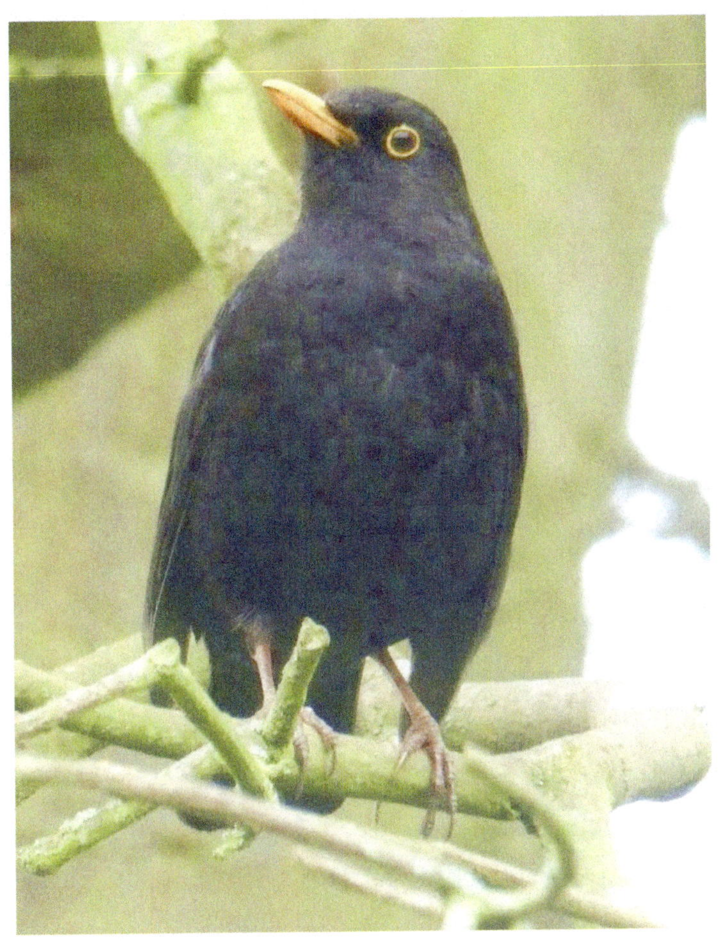

Sarah Dale

Lych Gate

A lych gate is a roofed gateway to a churchyard to where, before the days of undertakers, friends or family of the dead carried the body to await burial and might take the opportunity there to talk about the life of the deceased.

It was one September day.
Walking near Standon, we stopped for rest
and stared across the land to hills beyond.
Then, looking down, we saw not grass
but lines of silken webbing stretched across the field,
a low-slung criss-crossed canopy,
a gossamer veil over a green bed.
Those in the know will tell, no doubt,
of money spider woven threads.
But, for a moment, imagine:
that leaves from nearby trees in their descent
find here a brief, soft resting place
where May till Autumn gamut of green,
breeze led waltzes, tarantellas in the wind
and late fanfares of colour,
all are fondly brought to mind,
a lych gate of remembrance,
before they sink and merge with soil.

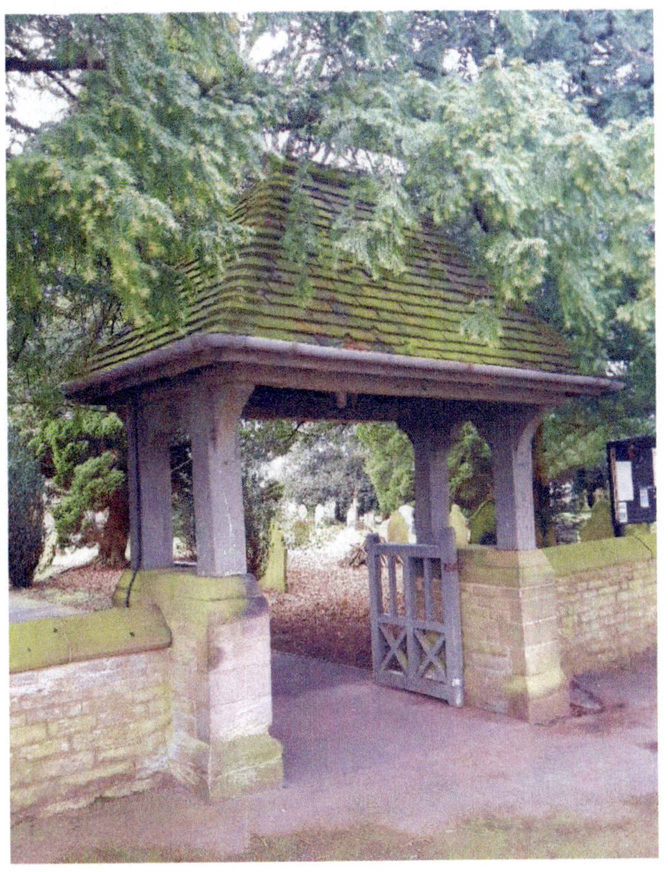

Lych Gate at a church on the Staffordshire / Cheshire border

Oliver Leech

Mister Toad

Oh what are you thinking
Mister Toad?
As you sit in the Staffordshire sun.
Statue like by the road,
where cars and tractors run.
Will you open your eyes,
maybe take a leap?
Or close them again -
after you've had a peep?
Perhaps you're waiting
Mister Toad,
for someone to come
near your abode.
Then in less than a second
you'll surely be gone
cleverly camouflaged
to everyone!

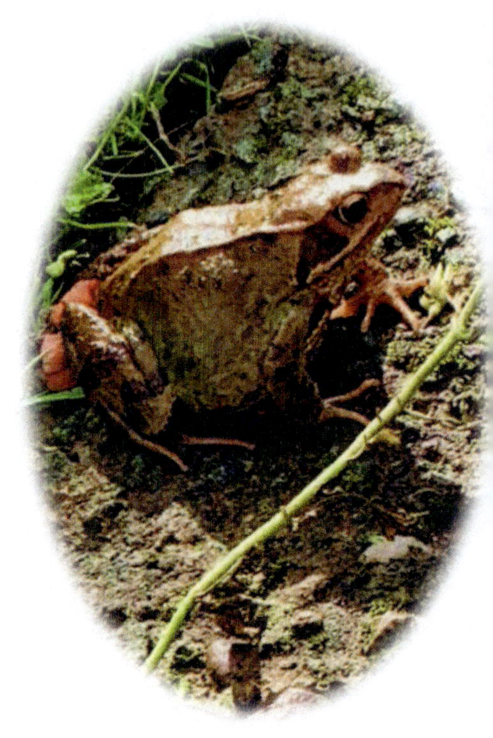

Anne-Marie Rowley

Oak Tree at Aqualate Mere

Stay close to me Oak
we lean up in all weathers
choosing our best path

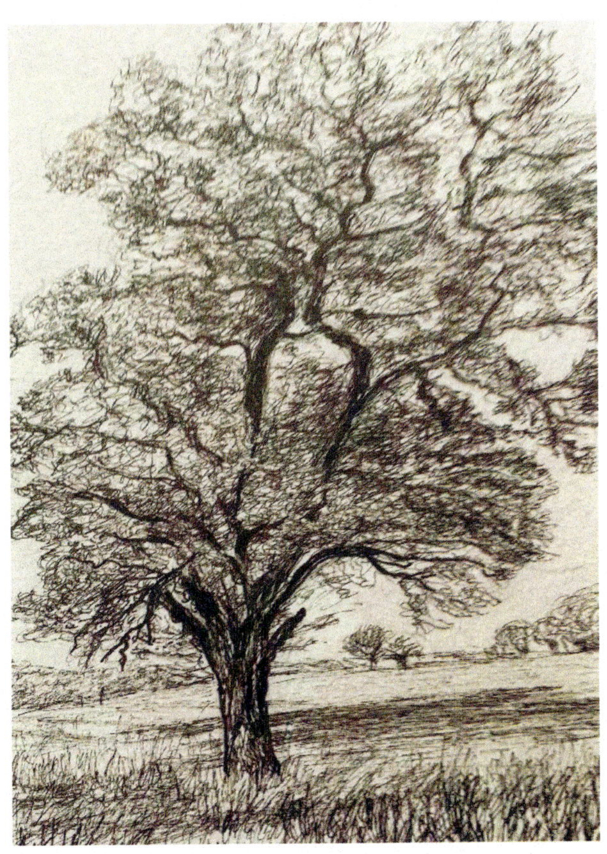

Oak Tree at Aqualate Mere

Netta Cartwright

On Brocton Bridleway

I've named you 'The Screaming Stump'

Standing solitary
betwixt fallow field
and bridle path
'The Screaming Stump'
a verdant vase full
of feathery ferns
feet shod in roots
of dock and grass
a soft sojourn
for a stone heart
proclaiming proudly
"The Brightest Star..."
Your furrowed shell
scarred by sorrow
left like lichen
on the tarnished brass
you, a *momento mori*
to their suffering
captured in nature's
carved scream

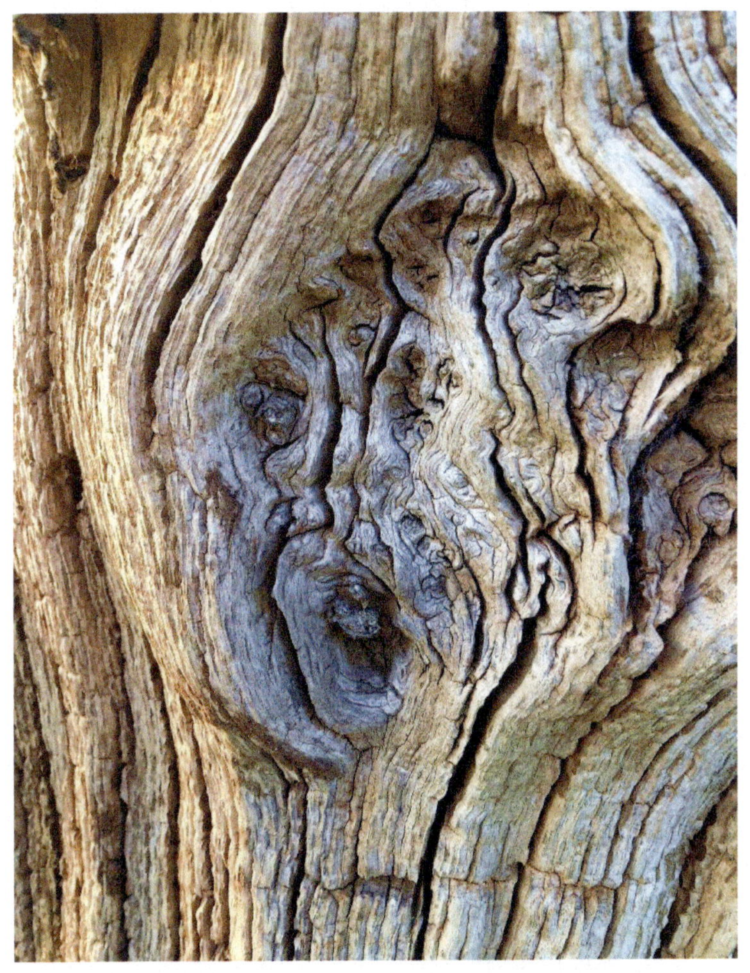

The Screaming Stump

Kathy Dowling

Our Waterways

Winding waterways,

twists and turns as far as your gaze,

parts of which resemble a chocolate glaze,

eerie in the early morning haze.

A moving motorway,

some might say,

of buoyant boats,

and others that float.

Frolicking fur and gliding feather,

out there in all types of weather.

Home to a floating community,

bringing together Staffordshire in unity.

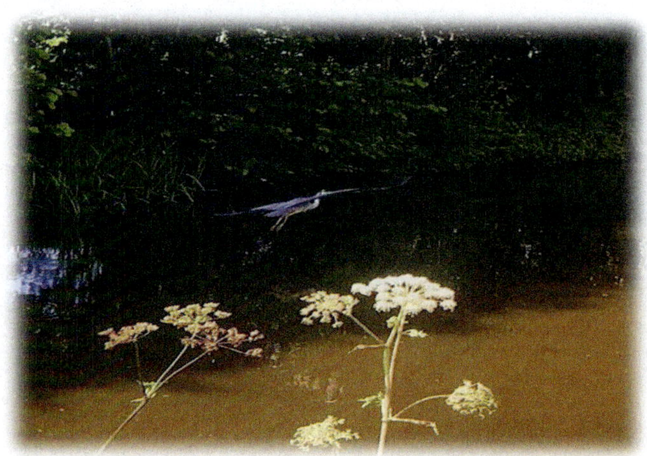

Daisy Corfield

Progress

Sunlight shafts through the sooty towers,
nourishing the grateful green grass,
noises float on the cool summer breeze,
over the wildlife corridor it'll pass,
carrying away pollen and some pollution,
from the distribution hub on mass.

Concrete with white painted lines my spot,
staring at a horizon blocked by progress,
fields of wildflowers between industries,
underneath heavy clouds that supress,
blackened by the towers' smoky emissions,
smothering life like a cheaply made dress.

Fences like barriers of iron stop trespassers,
replacing hedgerows where birds nest,
treated timber slowly rotting guard the sites,
dead wood pierced through and laid to rest,
planted between the islands of mother nature,
containing the squares of managed forest.

A monolithic street light watches over it all,
keeping the progress going on at night,
an artificial sun which never sets overhead,
confusing insects with its constant light,
altering ancient finely balanced food chains,
which could stop a species' progress plight.

All these white lines on the concrete we cross,
make a picture without the natural green,
forcing plants and animals into manmade sets,
idyllic oases of manufactured wild pristine,
thin corridors of walled freedom for all fauna,
takes the wild out of the wildlife I've seen.

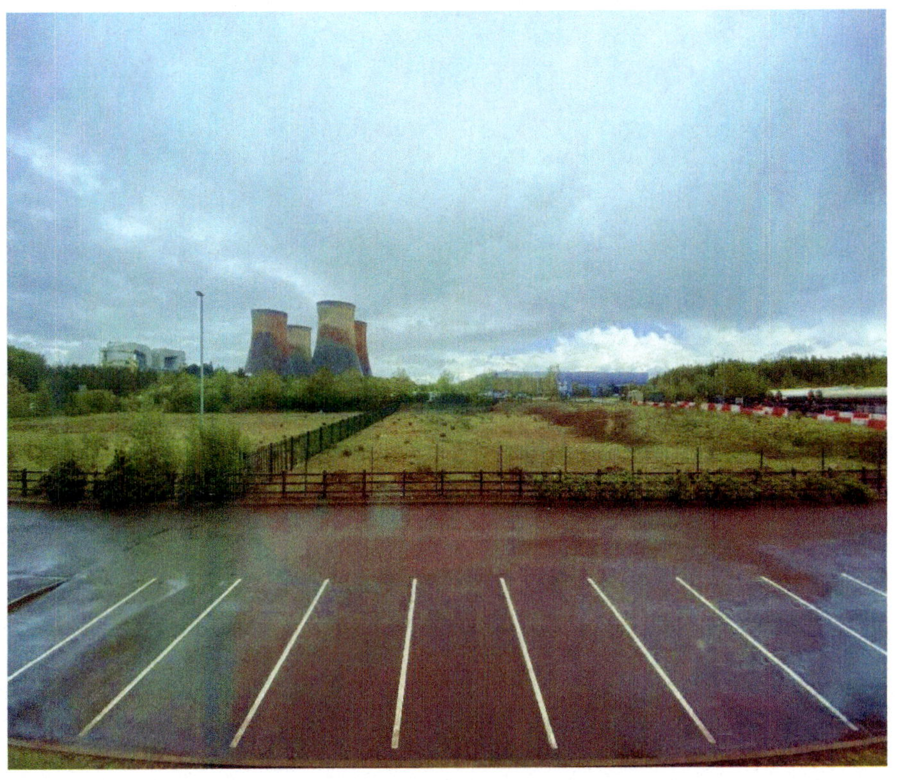

Rugeley Cooling Towers

Poem by Matt Gopsill

and Photograph by Adam Gopsill

The Common Plot

The sun shines low over a horizon of trees
branches sway and leaves rustle in the autumn breeze
the sky a canvas of pink and blue
the overgrown grass and the morning dew

cows huddled together to keep each other warm
the mud damp and soft, infested with worms
birds singing in harmony, far from the ground
crisp brown leaves falling, scattering around

rabbits return home to tend to their young
falling asleep to melodies the birds have sung
the meek little mole returns to his larder
curls up by his mate, falls asleep next to her

the pink and blue canvas turns inky with the night
stars speckled across the sky, shining bright
the flowers begin to close up their petals
the wind stops whistling and finally settles

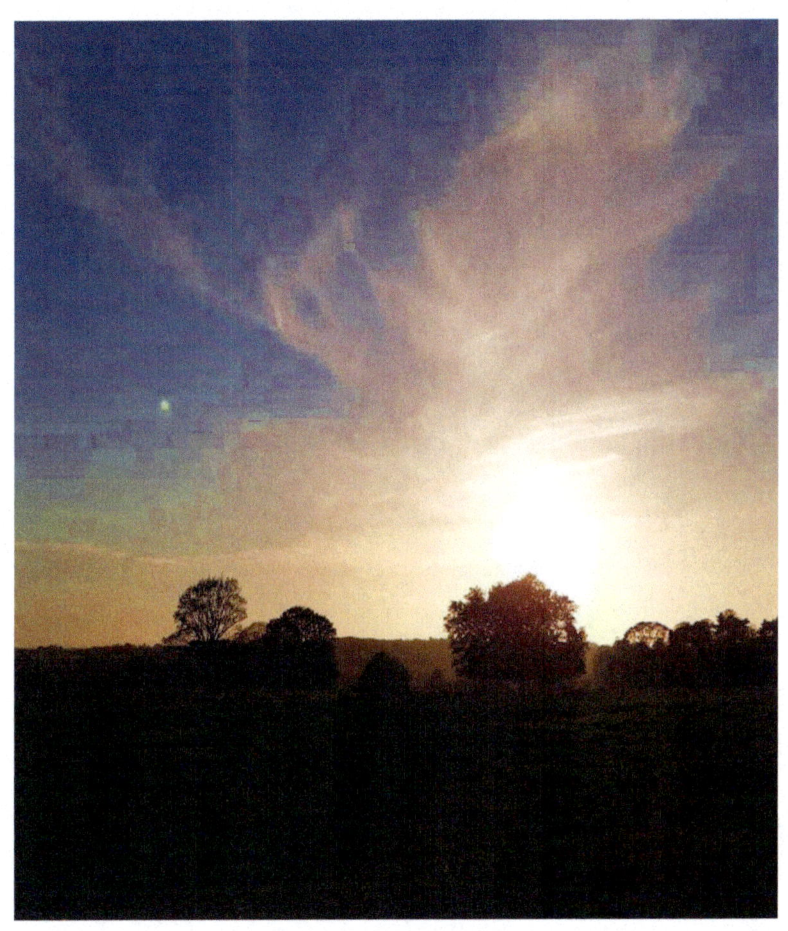

Staffordshire Meadow

Kayleigh Benbow

The Heron

Leave the stench of traffic at the main road.
Leave the brightly coloured traffic lights,
leave the noise and bustle,
and follow
winding pathways
down
to the river.

A scarcely coloured autumn day,
more grey
than mesmerising,
more brown
than ochre, orange and old gold
but by the tranquility of the river,
through the damp that strains my eyes
almost like
black and white dots on an old TV set,
I peer, and I see elegance.

Tall grey bird
stands statue like -
could be made of concrete until he turns his head…
Sharp beak glints briefly.
He shifts from foot to foot, uncomfortable, perhaps,

under our stare.
His reverie, interrupted.

Although we are silent,
he knows we are there.
He lifts his elegant wings,
graceful, almost lazy in motion.
He flaps once or twice, turns,
great wings power him forwards
almost at eye level.
Concrete feathers whisper past.

I admire the length of his body;
jutting breastbone,
straight beak, elongated legs
and piercing eyes,
as he flies up and away.

Through a tree,
over the road bridge,
he disappears until another day.

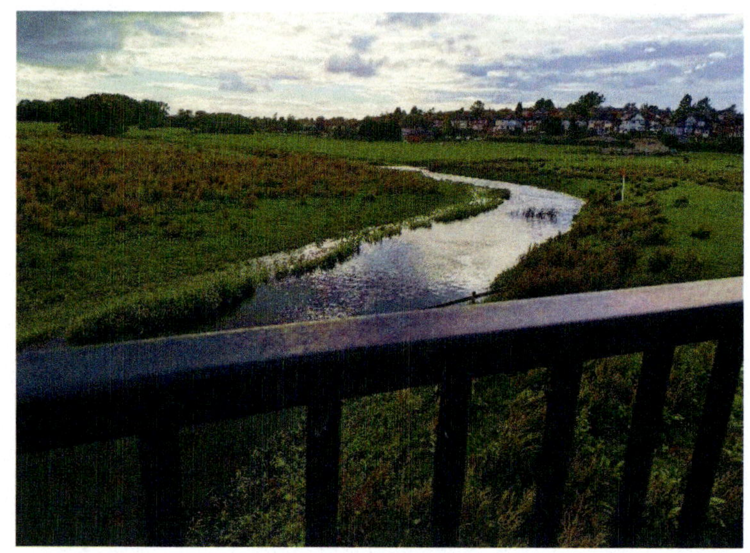

River Sow, Stafford

Mel Wardle Woodend

Staffordshire Poet Laureate 2019-2022

The Will of the Wind

A pepper pot figure
with such stance and vigour
how could it be
the plain brick rounds I see
once set sails to the sky
with a breeze in its eye
another lifetime
born to spin what was spun
to grind what was ground
with the will of the wind
powering it round

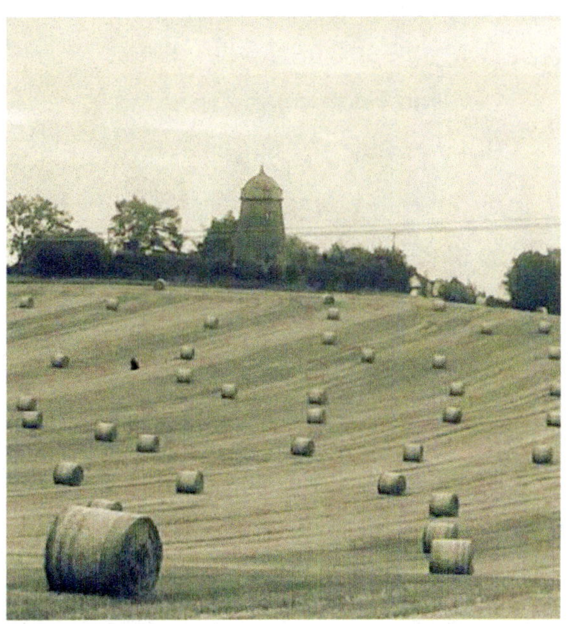

Amelia Reeves

Toadstool Temptation

At the edge of Bishop's Wood,
clustered in moist shade,
head heavy on stick torsos,
a phalanx of toadstools.
Plump and passive aggressive they sang:
'Pick me. Risk me.
Try me. Fry me.
Fly with me. Die with me.'
An alpha male in a single swoop
would scoop, snatch, swallow.
But I'm a lifelong danger dodger
made of timid stuff.
With just one backward glance
I walked on through the wood.
But were they poison
or once-in-a-lifetime portals
to places far, far beyond my geography?
Now I'll never know,
a thought to nag, to haunt me.

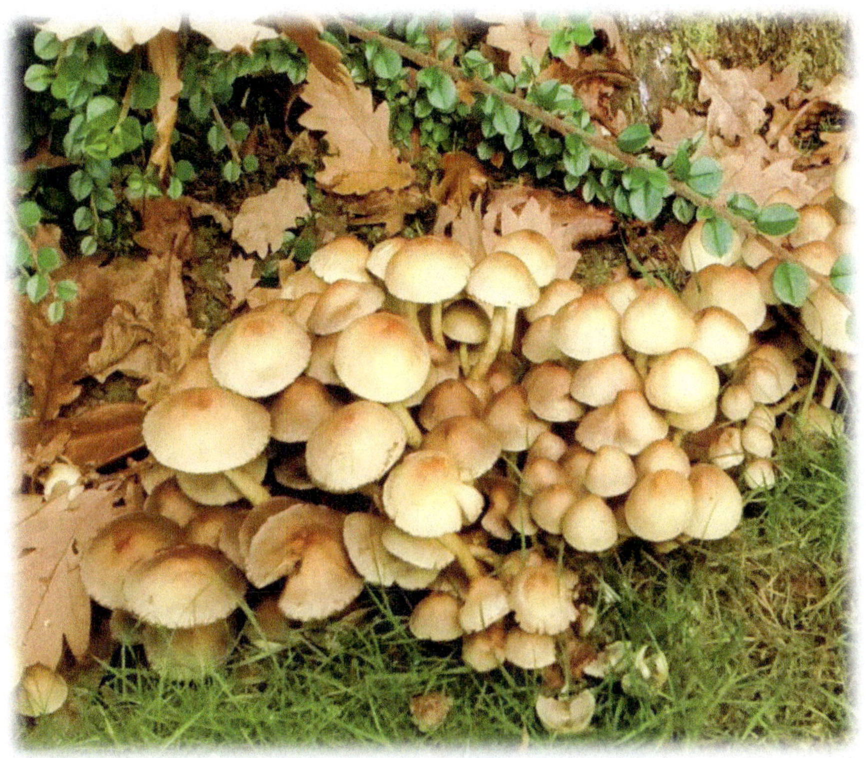

Toadstools at Bishops Wood

Oliver Leech

Tunstall Lightning Tree

I couldn't hear you
so I didn't see you.
Days, weeks, I walked on by,
no sense aroused at the scent
of your breath.

A catch of the wind
gave a sniff of a hint
of a life that once stood
proud, protective.

Now I can't look away,
my eyes are locked
on your immense majesty;
your stoic stature sings
with stubborn rooted apathy.

Your whispers barely murmur
as I creep closer through
overgrown grass, dodging empty
cans of Stella and hardened dog turds;
scent of rotting plastic on your breath.

Your leafless branches dance,
unafraid of death,
of lightning striking twice,
of lads with lighters
and phallic graffiti in mind.

I think, when they tattooed
your torso, when they trashed
your grave, that you stood
stock still and let them.

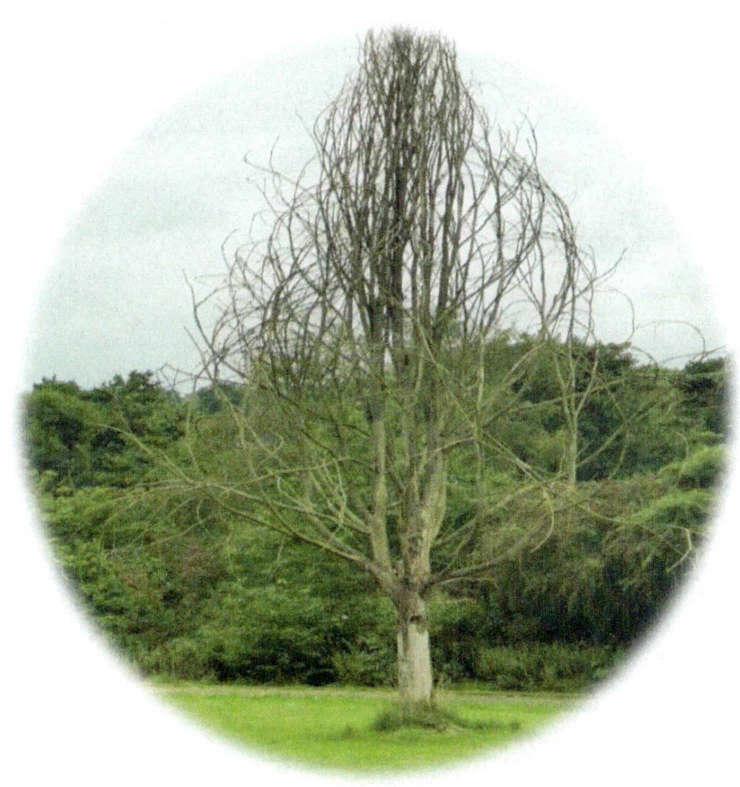

Ashley Edge

Tunstall's Lakeland Erratic

Look, Tunstall Park's erratic rock,
created deep within the earth.
This six-ton Lakeland granite block
was subject to volcanic birth.

For countless eons it just sat there;
the dinosaurs all came and went,
the rock remained without a care,
impassive and insentient.

Then came another mighty force
which scoured the earth and dragged the stone
until the ice age ran its course
and left it high and dry, alone,

sinking deep in Staffordshire clay.
It then was hidden from our sight;
men might not know that there it lay,
doomed never more to see day's light.

But when the lake was dug with spade
and pick, the stone turned up again,
then on its current site was laid,
and there it sits come sun and rain

its back and sides are rough and dark,
the sloping front is brightly burnished.
For decades kids thought it a lark
that with a slide they had been furnished.

(Until the information plaque appeared.)

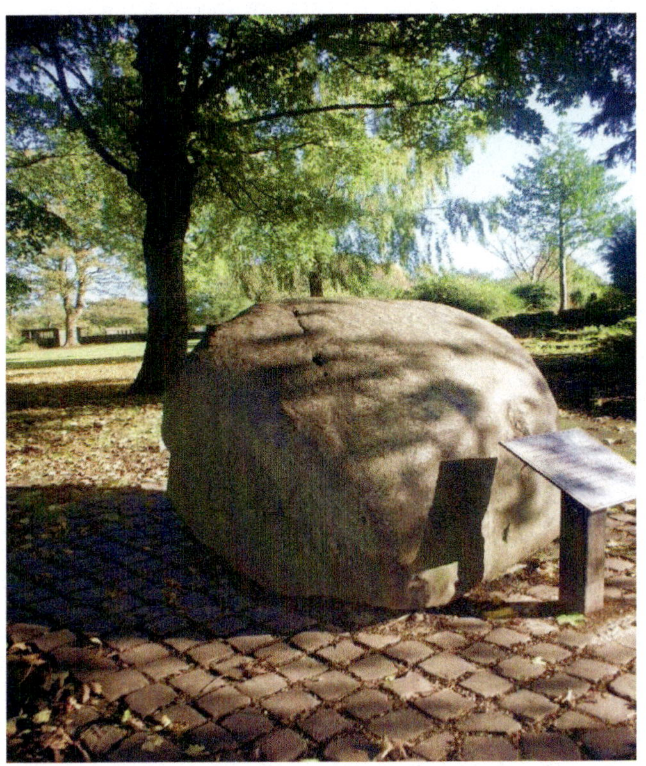

Malcolm J McMinn

PART TWO

PEOPLE AND PLACES

A Childhood Journey to Hednesford and Beyond

A window on the world from Whieldon's green bus
as we leave Rugeley with Grandma.
Field hedgerows fill up with bracken, then gorse,
as we near the dark bounds of the forest,
its interior mysterious, except to deer.

Hednesford camp. Hordes of grey-blue men hoof the stairs,
high spirited as horses; their caps at jaunty angles to impress.
Off duty chattering as they claim the bus.
Then on past the prefabs. Yet another camp,
where bare-foot children scramble in the dirt.

Rain falls as we wend our way through smoking heaps of slag;
like alien grey dragons, trucks crawling like fleas along their
spines,
dumping detritus from an unseen world.
And as we enter the town
wagons clatter under the railway bridge.

At the terminus the bus empties.
Crowds surge along the pavement to a chip-shop mecca,
where we are pushed into corners and we watch
as a boy eats chips off the mud-stained floor
amidst a host of trouser-legs and boots.

Our next bus trundles forward into Market Street.
Pungent smells of vinegar and damp wool permeate the air
As we climb out of the town and slowly up the hill.
Past a church where Gran whispers a prayer
Opening a window to another world.

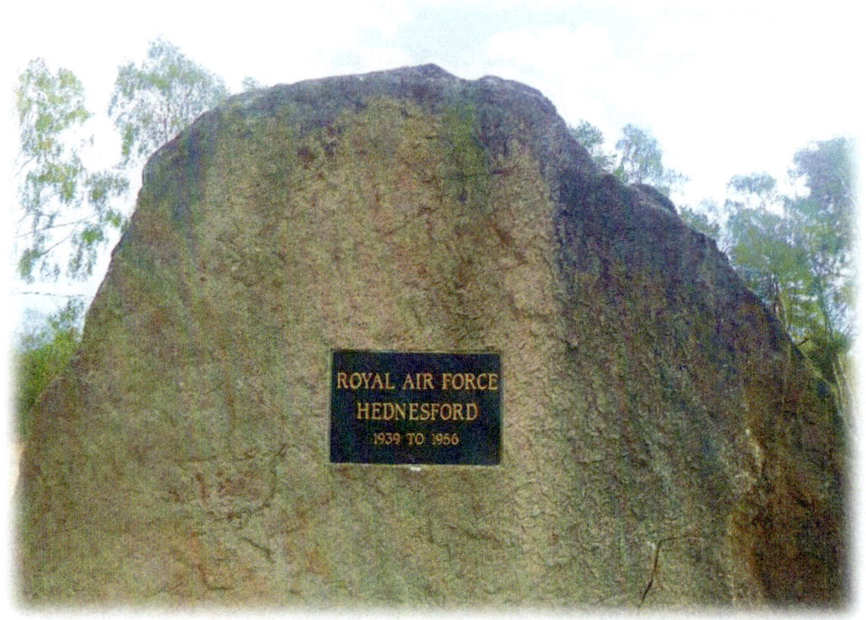

Hednesford Boulder

Pauline Hawkins

A Stafford Lass

with apologies to John Denver

Grew up with a plum in my mouth
so to speak
plucked from granddad's garden

1955 and now I am six
an only child but not lonely
we are all young families
on Highfields new estate

We skip, roller-skate, climb trees;
with dirty knees, ramble
through autumn fields
over to where the M6 will be come 1962

Into town on a Midland Red
Royal Brine Baths
Art Deco at the Picture House
chocolate box treats
and next door, posh frocks
at Madame Eugenie Moore

In the old market hall
we buy broken biscuits for dunking

Take me home, country roads

to the place I belong

over hump-back bridges

in the grey Ford Popular

butterfly stomach

"Do it again dad!"

I shout them out loud

the words

arms wide in a warm embrace

and hope he hears me.

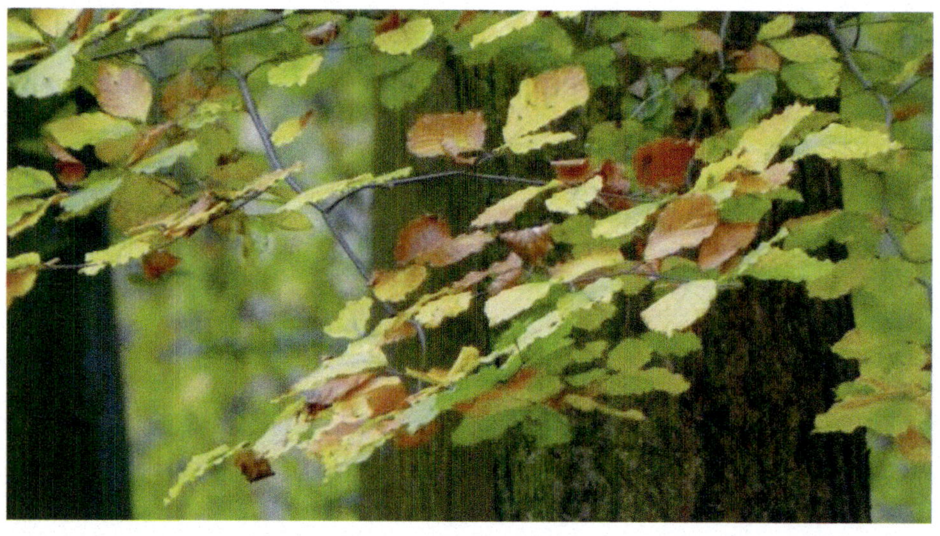

Daralyn Hammond (nee Benton)

Alton Towers at Autumn Time

The whooshing of the wind,
the wheels on the track,
where the summer sun dims,
and all the laughter comes back.

The ringing of the music,
the withering of the leaves,
the autumnal scent,
and the biting breeze.

The way the rollercoaster runs,
makes hearts leap with fear,
and yet we find ourselves queuing
for that pure rush of cheer.

Smiles brightening up faces,
and making eyes twinkle.
The adrenaline getting blood pumping,
and making faces tingle.

So many accents,
people from everywhere.
Many numb feet
from poor choice of footwear.

It is here I feel safe,
where I make new memories.
It is here I could stay,
for what feels like centuries.

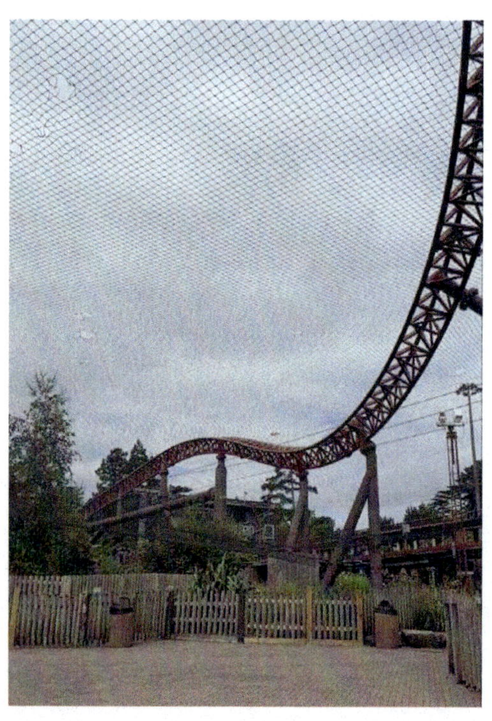

Ruby Weston

Cannock Chase Then and Now

As a child The Chase was an adventure playground
for me and my friends. It was a place for fun
and exploration where leaves, twigs,
bracken and broken branches were building supplies
for our dens. We crept along narrow paths
and undergrowth, collecting armfuls,
then returned to base to plan and place our spoils.

Once made we were free to sit, devise
secret codes and think of games to play.
Nearby, traffic spun past but we were invisible.
Dogs sniffed around but never found us.
We climbed trees, balanced on logs, ran
with abandon until nettles attacked.
But friendly dock leaves were always at hand
and stinging hives were our proud battle scars.

Decades have dashed by and I've moved
from hidey-holes of adventure, to appreciating
the riches of nature as I drive through an
ever-changing ancient woodland.
Pines, silver birches, beech and oak stand tall,
or bend and lean to the will of the wind and rain.
Wildflowers spring up when their season
arrives, to join bracken, brambles and holly.
Slow worms, grass snakes, adders and lizards find

homes amongst lichen, fungi and decaying wood.
Whilst common and rare birds forage, or fly
over fallow, red and muntjac deer
as they run across winding roads heading
to feeding stations, parks and gardens.

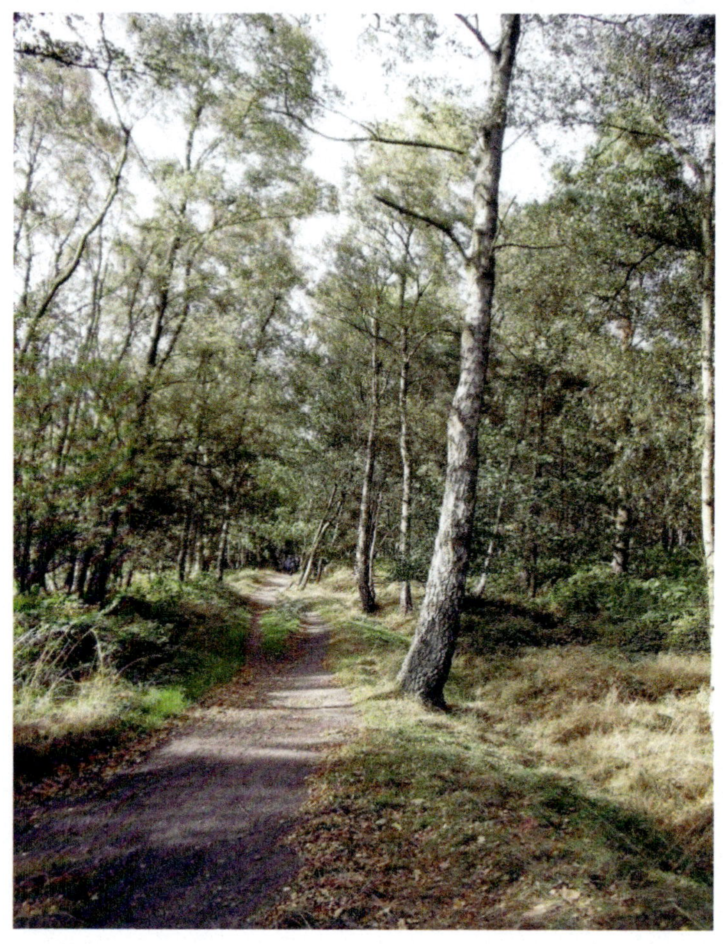

Janet Jenkins

Chisel

National Memorial Aboretum, Alrewas, Staffordshire

In this green heart of Mercia
climb the hill of grief and prayer,
looming walls of Portland stone
form the stark vision standing there,
shafts of sunlight lie in wait.

True the deadliest war long ended,
yet new names are carved with precision
for bodies blasted into oblivion,
chip, chip, chisel cleaves the silence
sharp white stone fragments fly.

Once armed forces, columns marching,
boots tramping, field guns pounding
bombs exploding, retreat sounding,
now ordered columns honour the fallen
in this garden of sorrow, a betrayal of peace.

Unceasing deaths, still millions mourn
haunting horror of blank stone walls
awaiting future desecration
more tears of anguish, more pools of blood
we stare at this abomination.

Chip, chip, chisel cleaves the silence.

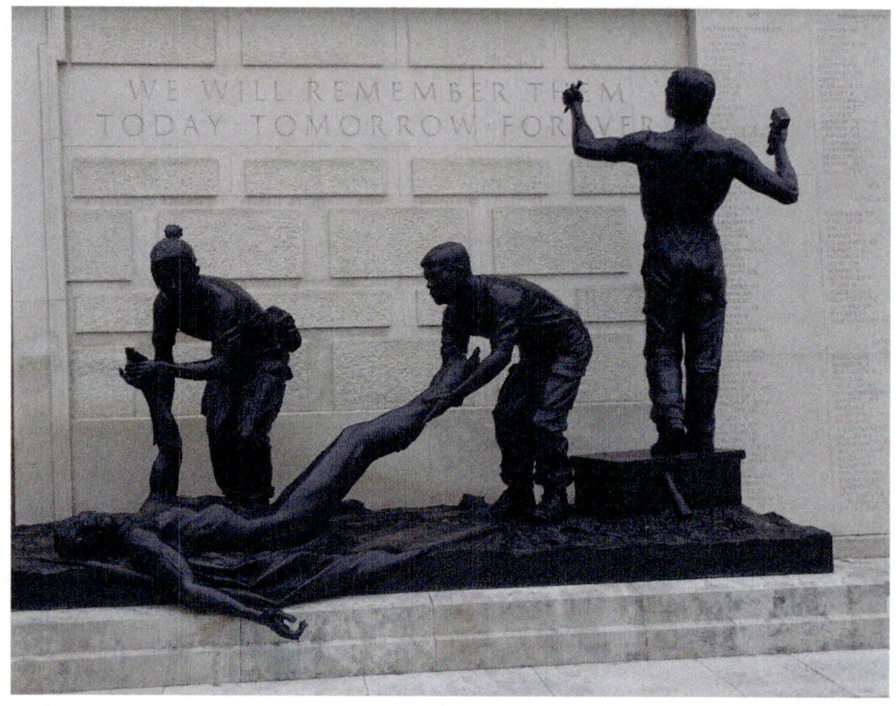

Sandra Mary Chambers

Dutty Wud

Coal's a dutty wud nah,
burrit allus woz a filthy joke.
It taks coal to shift coal, tha knows –

straight arta pit an int' firebox
barkin uz knuckles on't grate,
sparks in uz greasy caps,

big cylinders bangin away up front.
Good ole Charlie gizzus a push
an we lift 300 tons up t'hill.

Caverswall, Dilhorne an Blythe Brig
echo come wet weary mornins,
wek them colliers an pitboys

wi uz noisy, billowy clamber
over the valley top, draggin
Staffordshire's life-blood,

bringin jobs for poor folk who'd
elsewise have nowt. Gone nah, youth.
Pit's, tracks an coal all histry.

Nah an then, I fancy I can 'ear
shouts an cusses, see smoky towers
stretchin over Godley Brook.

But coal's a dutty wud nah!
So uz sit at 'om, turn up heatin'
check uz smartphone, watch telly.

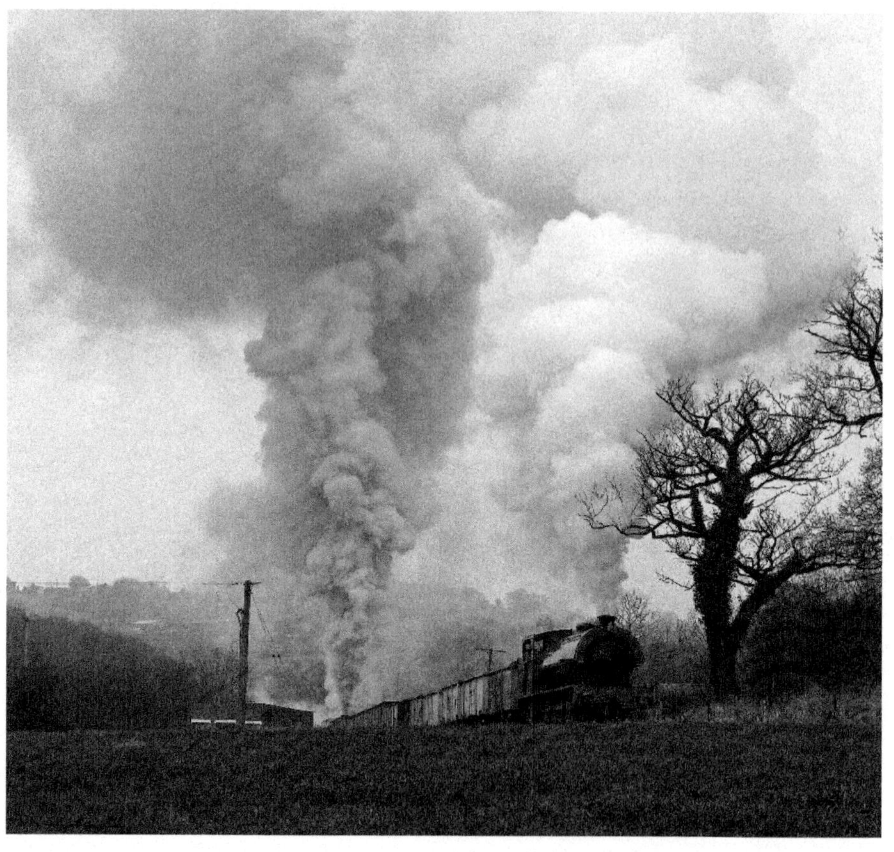

Phil Binding

First Rites Beyond Red Hill

Stone, North Staffordshire

Back here, what lies beyond this place, field, stream
and wood, is wilderness, intense, compared
to half-day-closed-all-week small market town
mean streets he wastes our early childhood in.
Long holidays are perfect clear blue skies,
enchanted time, off on his bike all day
with mates, the pedals proud against his feet,
on sunken winding tracks and bridleways,
down splashy Watery Lanes, the Downs beyond,
sublime, the prospect of no school for weeks,
till stifling afternoons oppress. Beside
himself, short fuses, bullying, ashamed,
he's pitching in, weird tingling deep inside,
dark chocolate bitter on his tongue, inspired.
Black clouds are gathering above Red Hill
like thunderheads: strange potions simmer in
the blood. The ladders yo-yo, pleasure – pain,
old nightmares stirred by rote, the snakes attract,
where parents, teachers, wield words-to-the-wise
like weapons, razorblades inside his brain.
Cheap perfume on the breeze, illicit pint,
prop cigarette, he's gazing longingly
at city lights some twenty stops away
projecting on the summer evening sky.
Raw promise of excitement, danger, sex,

he dreams of soft white flesh he's glimpsed above
dark stocking top beneath gyrating dress.
If we could charm dark energy to slide
beyond space-time the quantum way, what would
they make of me, d'you think? What could I say?

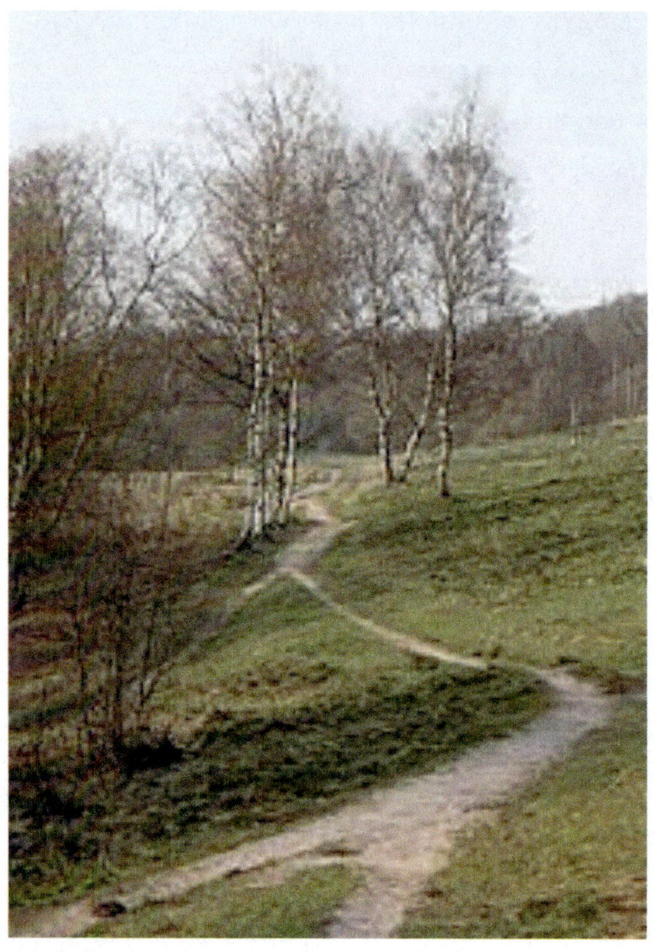

Peter Branson

Foundations

Two-faced
creased base
block built brutalism
corners the sky
with preform
fabrications
clean lining
the dream
of a new age
of architecture
Straight edge
flat roof
boarded
corrugations
reflect steel glint
solar flare
spotlights towards
distant ring road
ribbons
cutting through
historic buildings
Carvings of antiquity
Bordering
green space reserve
Trees
gilded with
red brick oxide
and rouge red
stop lights to Doxey
Our ancestors
look on
Their faces
carved by masons
hands and eyes
await the next
instalment
of relative progress

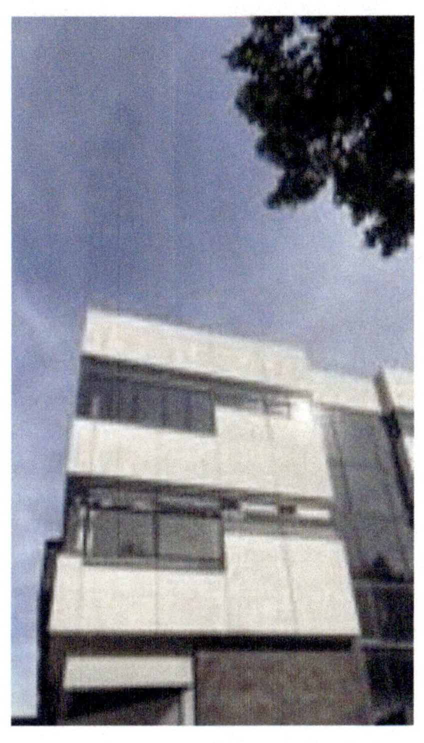

Brendan Hawthorne

German Military Cemetery, Cannock Chase

I follow the track from Broadhurst Green. Scent of pine needles imbibing me. Live, green, on living beings. Planted in rows, the irony not lost on me, as I stand above a shallow valley of roughhewn, grey granite headstones. Marking the dead, at rest.

A single wooden cross stripped of leaves it once gave birth too, its message clear to those who see beyond the canopy of green. Eyes cry the same tears, pain is indiscriminate in its deliverance.

I look back to war graves of France and I feel the loss and grieving in both. Sleeping, the deepest sleep.

Under the same stars, the same waxing moon that halo's a ghostly barn owl and night creatures scutter in its deepening shadows.

Under the same sun, in clearings, where trees have been coppiced to allow its warming glory to warm butterflies' wings.

In the same breeze that cools foreheads of walkers, like a travelling fox following trails through the heathland.

In the same rain that nourishes new grass each spring, for rabbits to silflay in a tale of Watership Down.

Each in each other's homeland.

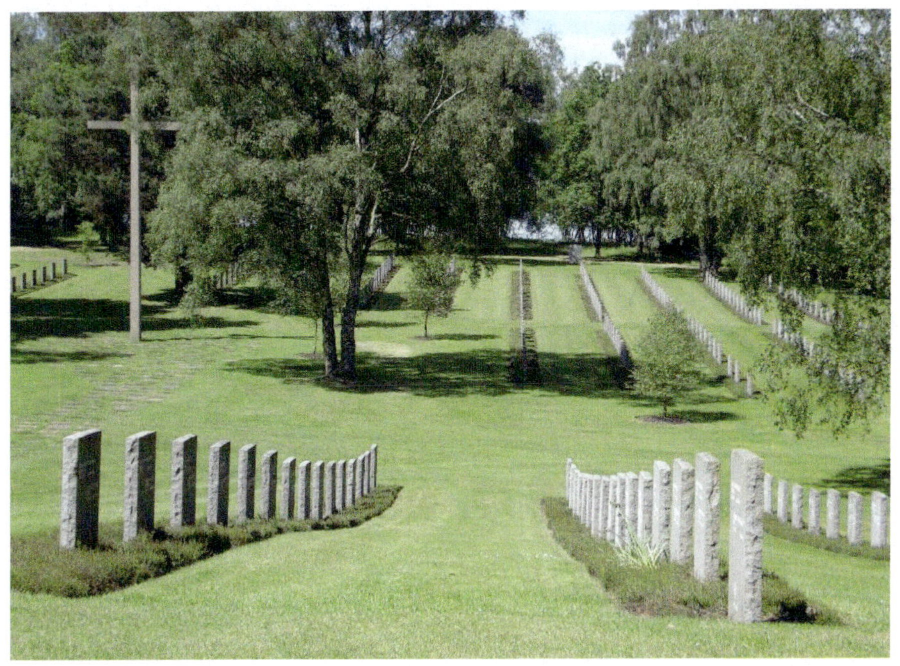

Jan Hedger

"Half Return to Stafford Please"

I lied,
I told my mum and dad that I was going to the library,
the perfect alibi for me.
I liked to read.

I walked,
then caught the bus straight into Stafford, coins in clammy hands,
giddy with rebellion.
I was always good.

I ran,
blurring black and white buildings, stumbling on cobbled streets.
Past swaggering pigeons,
seconds tripping by.

I stopped,
marched with purpose to the gift shop that used to be behind the church,
with money saved from Grandma,
I purposefully perused.

I bought,
a present for my best friend, Michelle, she was leaving Middle School.
A friendship bracelet, in a box.
To help her remember.

I returned,
jostling jubilantly on the bus, amidst strange faces,
clutching my treasure,
watching fields reel by.

I lied,
I told my mum and dad that the library had been fine,
that I'd bumped into Abbie,
and we'd lost track of time.

Sorry I lied.
But Michelle did love the bracelet.

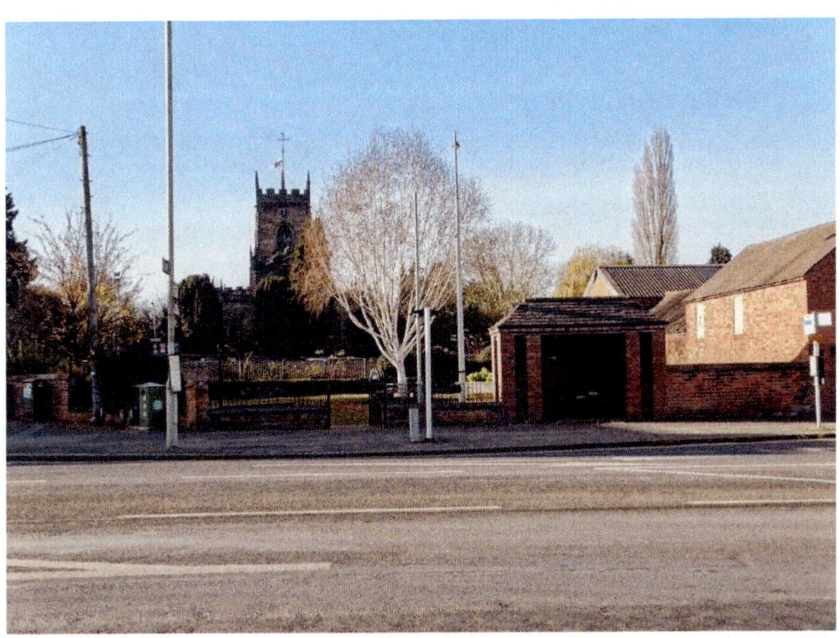

Poem by Rebecca Banks (now aged 40)
Photograph by her dad, Mark Roberts (all is forgiven)

Hanford Roundabout

Hanford's just a Roundabout,

but it wasn't always so,
I was born and bred there many years ago.

My eyes first saw the ocean blue in Hanford bluebell wood,
I carried home great armfuls as often as I could.

The river Trent went rambling through, beneath the bridge, as now,
and watered war-time carrots, in allotments down below.

My father took us nutting in the leafy lanes around,
returning home to shrieks of joy at bounty we had found.

His big hands rubbed the barley grains to give us milky seeds
we sucked on purple clover found among the weeds.

We hunted pig nuts, good to eat, picked blackberries from hedges,
the Banky Field in winter was alive with speeding sledges.

The Banky Field had castles too, and towers with princesses,
gallant knights upon white steeds, to climb their golden tresses.

The farmer had a horse field where we stopped to say hello,
to stroke his velvet nose and lips, and feed him apples - with the pips!
Which made our progress slow.

A cockerel high and mighty swung above the church,
crowing, creaking in the wind, to make the stomach lurch.

The tuck shop on the way from school held sweet delights - how many!
Some for just a ha'penny, and plenty for a penny.

Pink spearmint bars, sherbet dabs with liquorice sticks.
Black jacks, and fruit gums, Mum,
red tipped cigs to burn your lips.

The Michelin Man rolled in a hundred years ago,
to point in the direction we were all to go.

Now Hanford is a Roundabout,

St. Teresa's still on site,
protecting all who circle round, busy day and night.

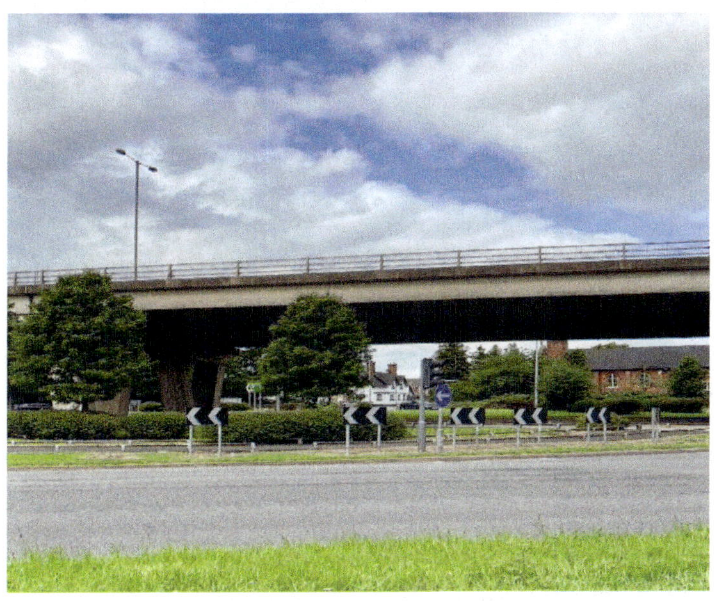

Bel Crawford

In Praise of Staffordshire Oatcakes

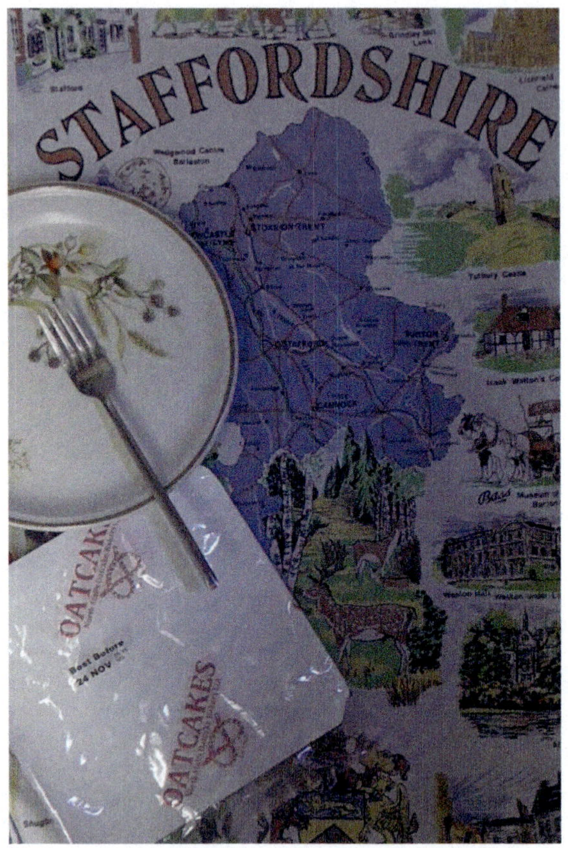

Soft and round and tasty
they're an absolute delight
I could happily eat oatcakes
every day and every night

They're also very versatile
with a sweet or savoury filling
spread it on and roll 'em up
(after a bit of grilling)

Grate some cheese and chuck it on
then grill a little more
until it's nicely melted
you'll eat them by the score!

Sweet fillings are just yummy
Maple Syrup is for me
I have three or four for breakfast
washed down with a mug of tea

If you're catering for others
want to serve up something posh
a fruit and whipped cream filling
makes a proper tasty nosh

Right, now to take the photo
of some oatcakes that I've got
Oh! This poem made me hungry…
So I ate the bloomin' lot!

Jane James

Lunch with Vera

We're side by side. Brief
breathing-space, busy working
day. What would you say –

I ask, (but quietly,
knowing what they do to those
who talk to ghosts) – what

would you say if your
cold, still form should thaw and wake?
What would you make, of

this weary, wounded
world? Of death, heaped up,
remembering: last

gasps, cold seas, quick blades,
a policeman's hands
or knee, flood, war, plague –

What would you say? All
that you worked for, turned to dust.
You must despair, grieve,

believe us to have
lost the lessons you learned, turned
our backs on goodness,

hope and peace. You speak,
at last, (or, perhaps the trees
move in the breeze.) - Look.

Look up. Turn your face
to the sky. Love, truth, beauty
never die. Go on.

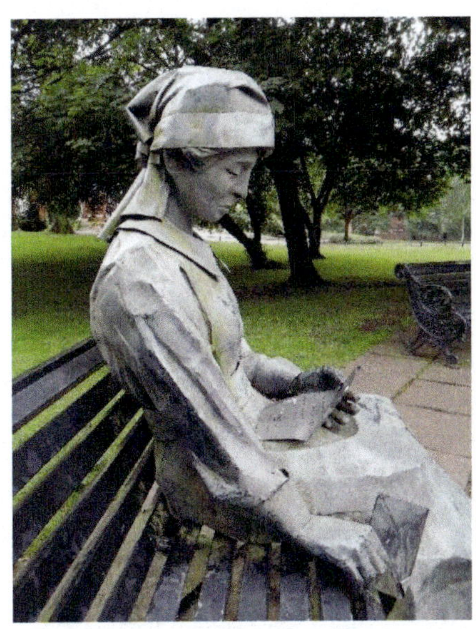

Notes on the photograph: The photograph is of the Lady in the Park, a sculpture by Andy Edwards, which is sited in the Brampton, Newcastle-under-Lyme. The sculpture was inspired by writer, feminist, socialist and pacifist Vera Brittain, who was born in Newcastle.

Tracy Smith

Massacre

Outstretched eagles' wings. Perched above back granite.
Letters inlaid in gold. No names, only numbers 22.000 souls.
Brave Polish military heroes. Interned prisoners trapped between the Russians and Germans.

On one fateful day in 1940, they were dragged to the square in Katyn, Western Russia. Shot in the head, shoved into a mass grave.

When you take your stroll, take time to pass through the cemetery.
Pause at the fitting memorial, place your hand on the black granite and close your eyes.

In silent prayer, remember the unknown, the forgotten Polish who joined us
in the fight against tyranny.
For FREEDOM.

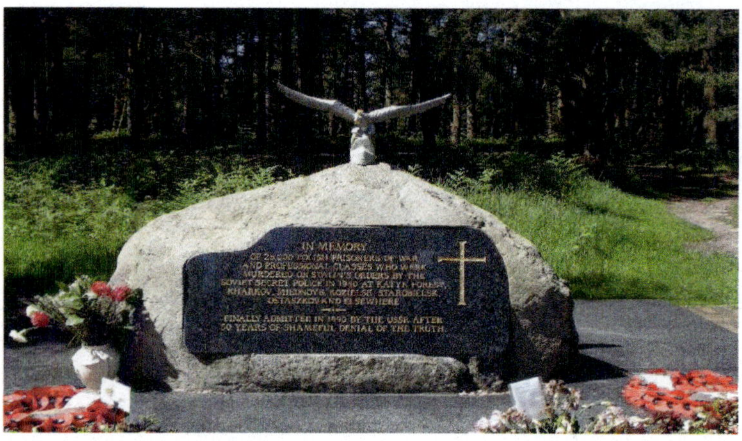

Pauline Faulkner

Memories of Early Lane

Memories of Early Lane
the Sun came up and went down again
where children played till it was black
and curtains moved and then shot back

Mrs P lived on the corner of our street
and in her back garden there were flaking painted seats
where we carved our names and we thought up all our silly games
we didn't have much but we loved it just the same

Hobnail boots on tarmac lane
let us know he was home again
with pence in pocket we would go
up the road to see Charlie and Flo

Mrs P lived on the corner of our street
and in her back garden there were flaking painted seats
where we carved our names and we thought up all our silly games
we didn't have much but we loved it just the same

Headmaster strict but he was fair
with cane in hand and icy stare
post lady now with named street
pushing bike her hair so neat

Mrs P lived on the corner of our street
and in her back garden there were flaking painted seats
where we carved our names and we thought up all our silly games
we didn't have much but we loved it just the same

These are memories of .... Early Lane

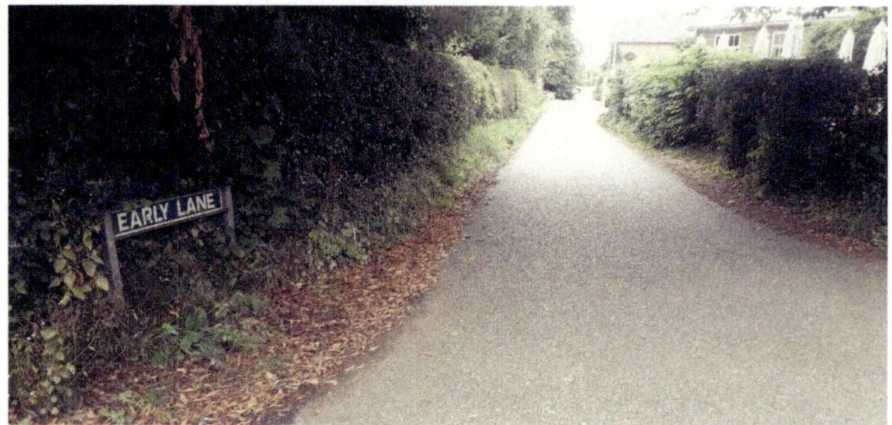

Ian Challinor

Mistral Dew (almost)

Being human kind — a would-be poet writes — *conjoins us all*
with fragile threads almost invisible and pure
and when a single strand is cut I feel the loss;
my intellect reacts; my body resonates;
the feeling is that I in some sense
have become the less.

John Donne's sermon still resounding like a peel of bells;
although long gone his Polesworth lines live on
to be repeated to distraction by a generation
which has never even heard his name;
which doesn't know his humble/noble place of birth.

As Jung explained the intellect is just
one function (some say fiction) of the human soul;
not a wholesome bigger mirror — more like tiny fragments;
little bits of silvered glass held up in innocence
by infant minds in expectation that
the incandescent sun becomes bedazzled.

What's stone gold true for one
may seem deluded through another's scope
but while we are connected threads
we can debate, agree to disagree or fight or flee
or pause and read some words — upon a trail
a poet took to heart — that prick the intellect
and/or stir the unassuming soul.

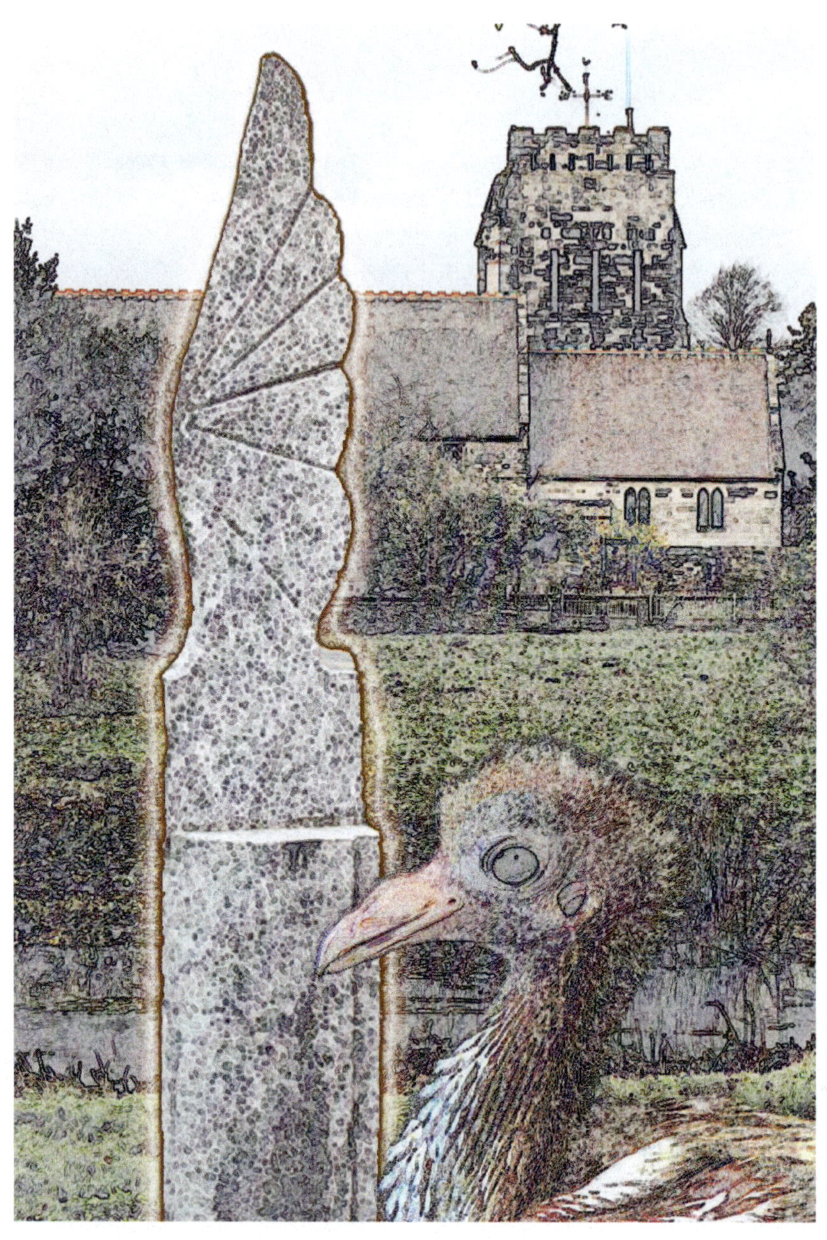

John Carpenter

On the Map

I live in a town,
in a city, in a county,
in a country that daren't
put us on the map.

As if we are not larger than life,
as if we have not
the potential for
greatness.

I stand on the hills
in sonder,
while London
thinks not of us.

Patchwork fields of jade,
jaded by ignorance
and trodden
by Forgotten feet.

Everyone agrees to leave
before their breath,
but sees not the uncounted seeds
that will stay beneath the earth.

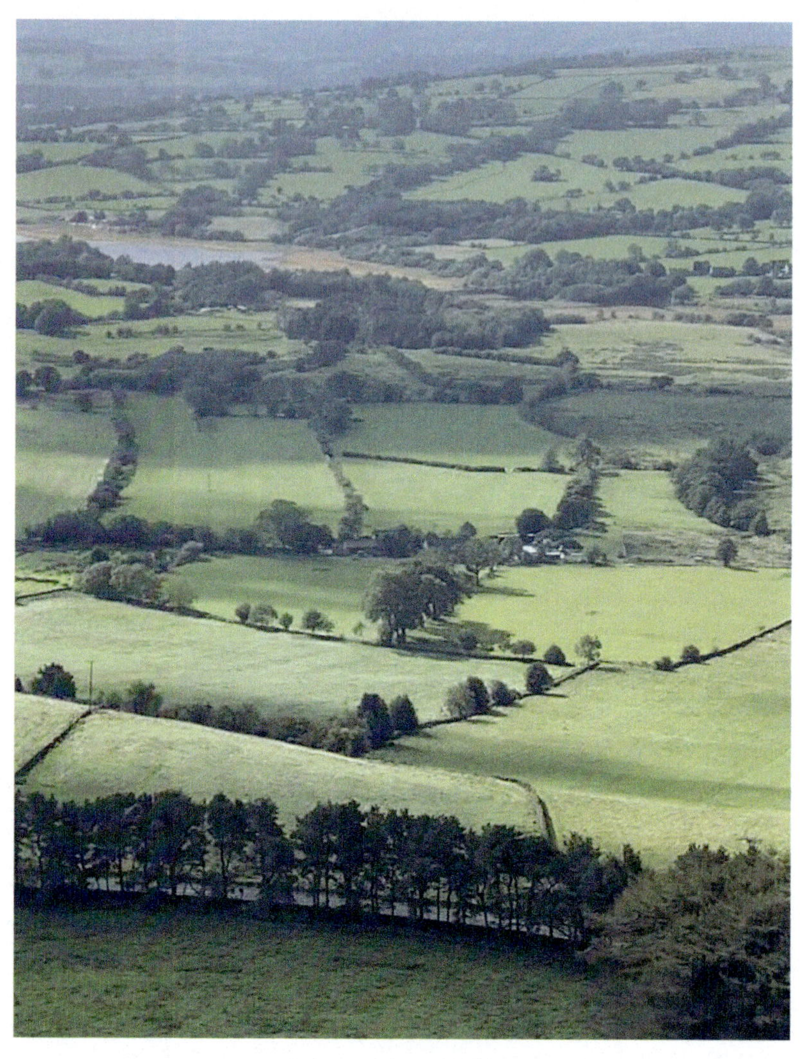

Erin Gascoigne-Jones

Staffordshire Young Poet Laureate 2021 - 2022

Paper Plane

Floating through the Staffordshire sky,
my paper plane glides gently by,
reaching up towards the clouds,
gliding over the miniscule crowds,
admiring the beauty beneath its wings,
as the sound of nature sings,
diving through trees of pine,
just above horizons line,
in the distance looking down,
lies the gem of Stafford town,
ancient history meets modern lives,
shows Tudor buildings still survive,
whizzing back through the trees,
my paper plane returns back to me.

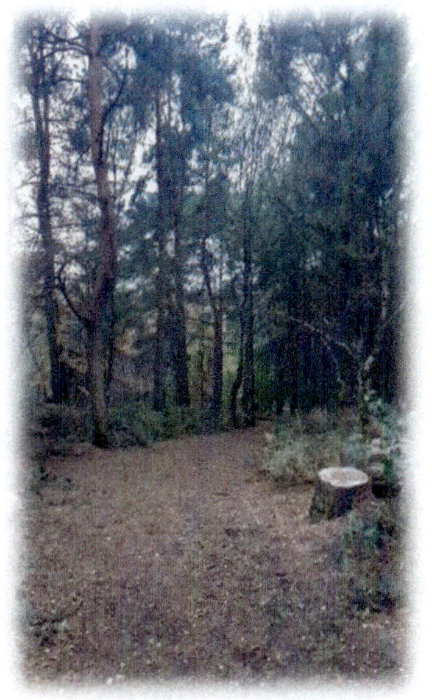

Holly Molsom

Pipe Dream

Clouded in smoke
mum in the front passenger seat
me in the back
singing
dad at the wheel
puffing
the smell of tobacco
comforting
like the salty taste of the skin
on his dear pate
when I kiss it

Milford
Brocton
Penkridge
home via Hyde Lea

Dad is never parted from his pipe

At the theatre
in the interval
he is up and out
into the street to puff
[always a gentleman
never smokes indoors]
returns with pipe stuffed in pocket

Act two
resettled in the front stalls
a dig in the ribs from a stranger
"Excuse me, mate, I think you're on fire!"
Unscheduled entertainment
an extra
we were not expecting…

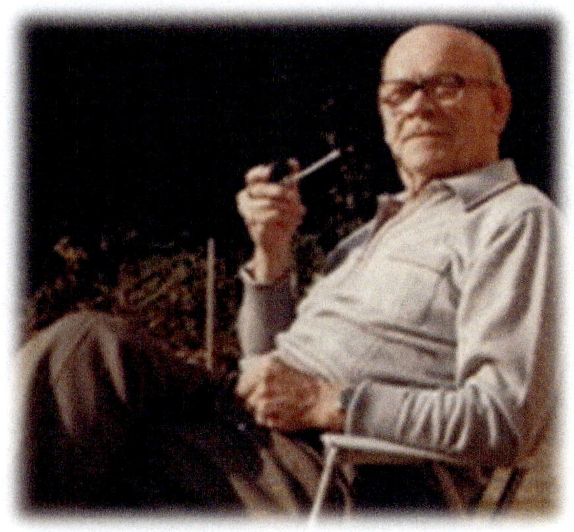

Daralyn Hammond (nee Benton)

School Trip to Doxey Marshes

Skipping down to Doxey Marshes,
hats, coat, boots on,
all wrapped up and ready to go,
teachers nagging us to leave
students chatting all the way there.

Jumping in all the muddy puddles,
stomping on the crunchy leaves,
hearing the rustle under my feet,
walking in the autumn breeze
the air as cold as a freezer.

Our breath like foggy ghosts escaping our bodies,
fingers stiff like planks of wood,
soggy feet squelching in our wellies,
everyone's nose and check were as red as blood,
teeth chattering whilst we try to talk.

Students' excitement rises as we draw near,
teacher telling us to stay calm,
stand still, in front of us,
a massive place with green and brown grass,
it was Doxey Marshes.

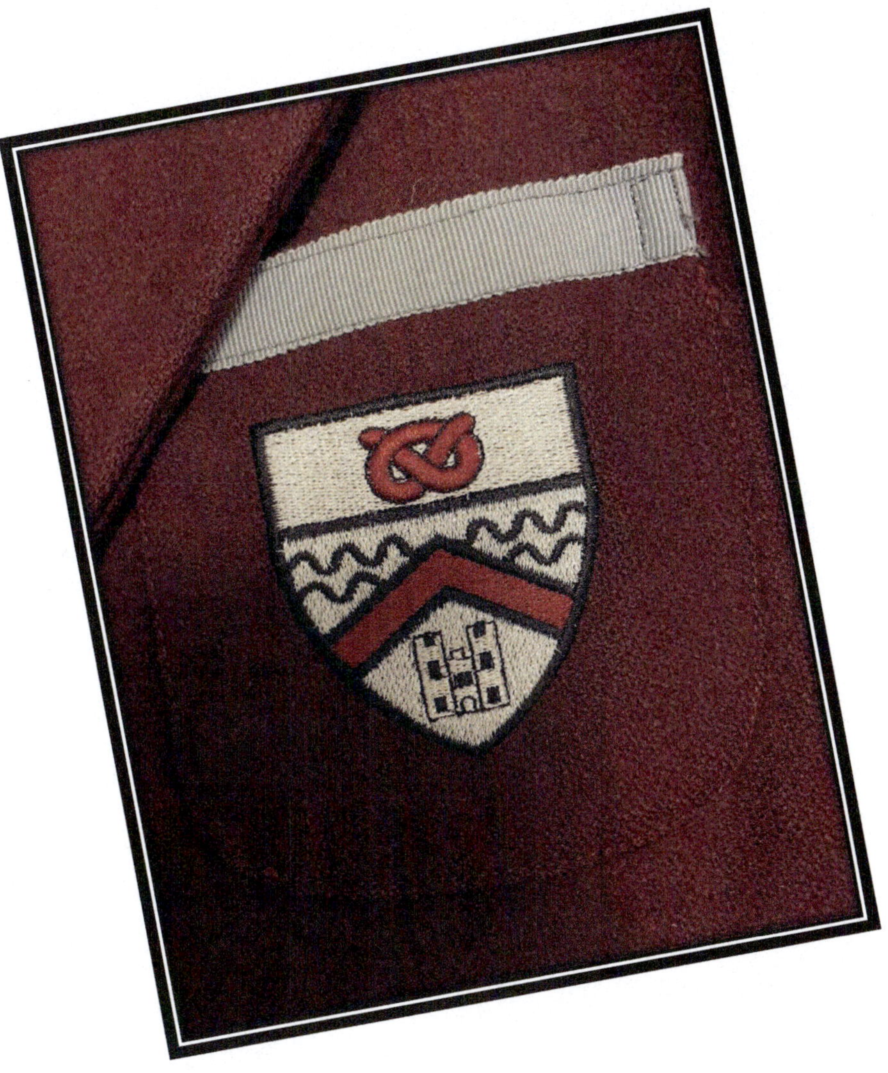

Lucy Wakefield

Stafford Castle

Many lives, many faces, drawn across the timeless ages
of women and men, of warriors and lovers
wood turned to stone, now ruins once a home
of towers and turrets and tunnels and tiles

The belly of the mound it rests upon holds secrets of its own
the moat sits as a wound carved out by man who shaped the land
old woodland trees stand tall as guardians where villagers once stood
well-trodden paths link ties to community, family and tribe

If walls could talk, what tales would they tell?
Walls… tell me of the sharpest of arrows flying from your eyes
tell me about the deep cries of invaders carried upon the wind
tell me of the ascent of battle on your slippery slopes

The castle lays silent.
Yet if you listen intently at twilight,
you'll hear the sound of craftsmen carving their wares from trees left behind
inhale deeply at sunset to smell the aroma of cooking pots whose shards lie buried beneath us
gaze softly through a keyhole at dusk to see the trail of a velvet dress sweep the winding stairs

glide your fingers along the cold bare stone in the dark of night to feel the scars from swords of iron

fall asleep in its keep and dream of native tongue whispering words of days gone by

and awake at dawn to bare witness to the sun breaking across the vast skies of Mercia,

with the same awe as our ancestors once did.

And I wonder… what stories of old truly lie forgotten here?

Shh, these castle walls will never tell.

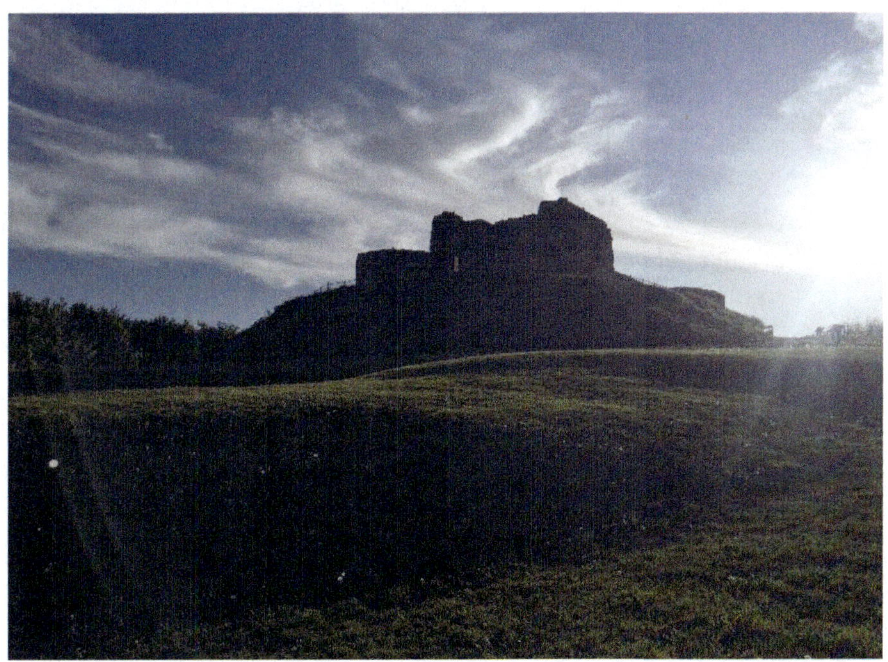

Lindsay Adams

Stafford Castle

Despite the darkness

staring down from history

you lift my spirits

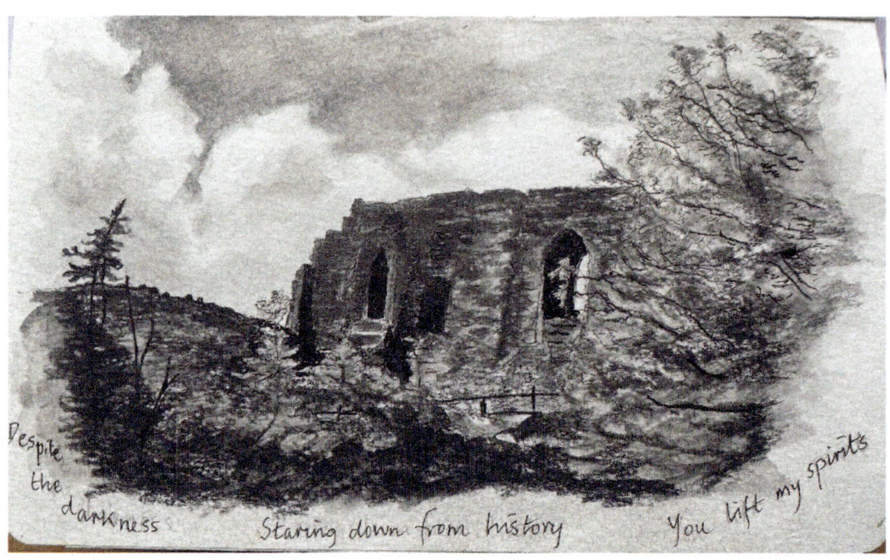

Netta Cartwright

Staffordshire

The canal tow paths twist and wind
it is so peaceful most people find
but 100 years ago the noisy shires towed the boats
and the pottery never broke
Wedgewood built those canals 1759
so that the beautiful pottery could one day be mine
the money made was used to build a community
but poverty was a living cruelty
people didn’t earn enough in other parts
and its pottery meant that we could restart
because our society lost so many in the mines before.

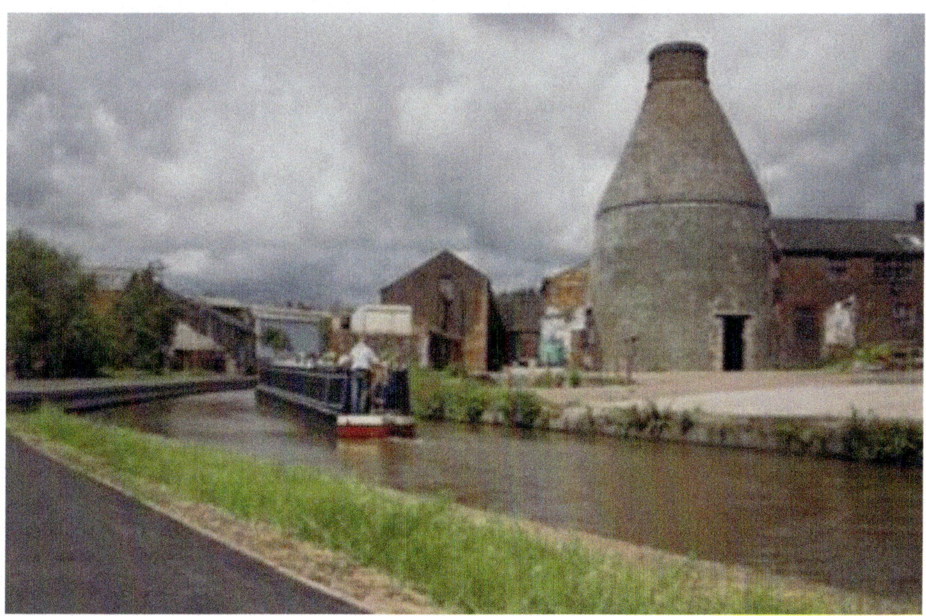

Molly Dobson

Sugnall Walled Garden

I watch as you sit there
and long to sit beside you.
You're smiling in the sunshine,
amongst the apple trees,
basking in the blue sky.

I see you immersed in the beauty.
At peace in your happy place.
Laughing and chatting with Dad.
Watching your grandson chase the ducks.

The scent of rhubarb signals spring.
As the butterfly glides from plant to flower.
A sea of lilac entices the bees.
As flame coloured fish swim.

In the autumn we huddled together,
shivering in the damp,
as the leaves turned, gold, copper, and bronze.
The pumpkins ready to carve.
The children splashing in the puddles.

What is our purpose now?
We come to remember,
to sit in the stillness,
to gather as a family.

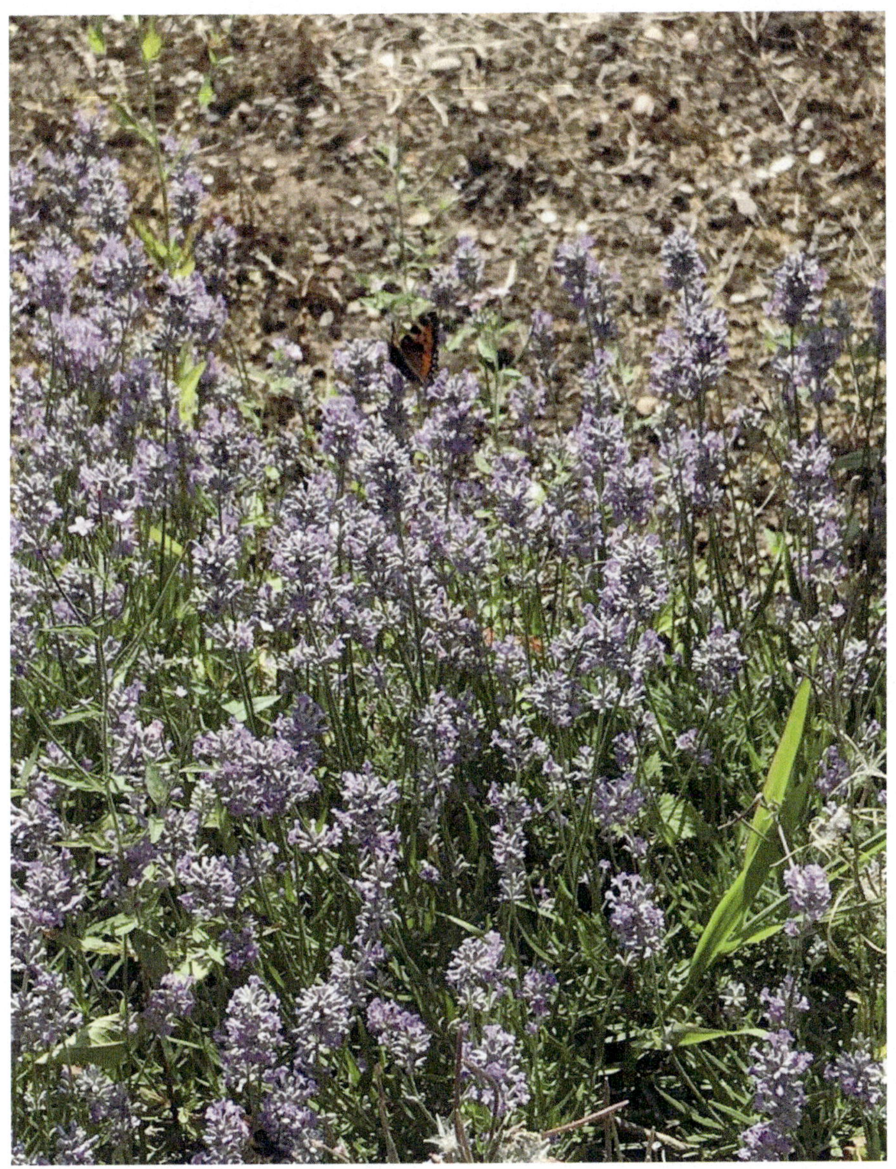

Victoria Lister

The Canal

The long winding canal
that runs through many towns
it stretches for miles
and takes a while to walk

The locks separating each section
so nice to watch the open and close
letting each barge through one by one
so they can carry on their journey along the long winding canal

The canal sight,
countryside to industrial
each section different from the rest
at some points, farmlands
and at others, factories

This is what Stoke – on - Trent evolved around
a long time ago
from one end to the other of the city

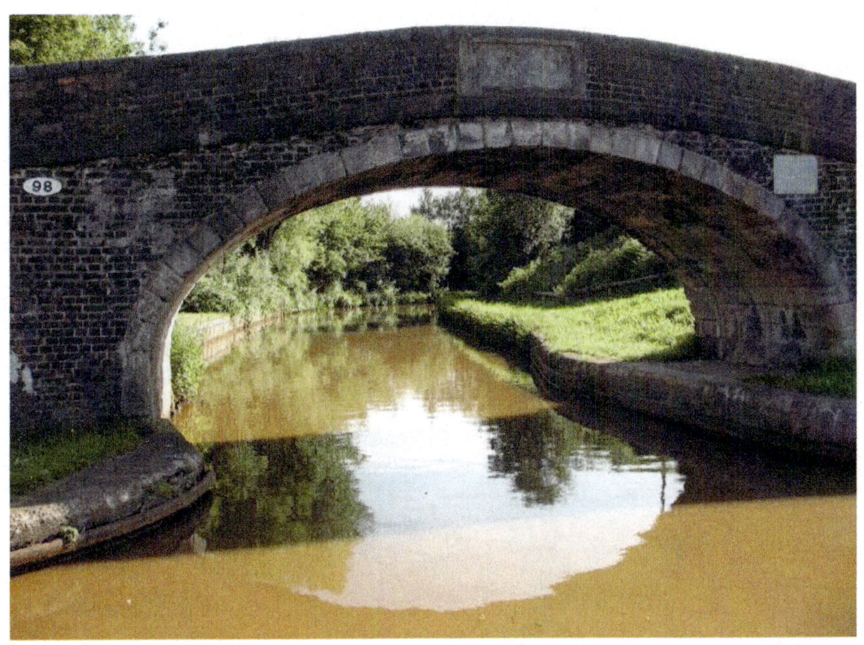

Rebecca Forster

The Island

There is a place,
almost impossible to reach,
hidden by a vortex of spiral pathways,
an island without a beach.

A secret nation separated by,
an impassable dead black moat,
and an army of knights,
with blinding red lights.

Once entered into orbit,
of lanes, arrows and banners,
the unhelpful white signs,
of sadistic town planners.

"Which way to go?" we stare in a daze,
enemy vehicles and labels everywhere,
extreme graffiti of North & South,
confused roadworkers once named it 'Nouth'.

Here we go round the Mulberry Bush,
circling and gyrating over again,
forced into trajectory once more,
following the wrong stripy lane.

When finally we enter,
after a string of right-turns,
vet, MOT and paneer,
exit warp speed top gear.

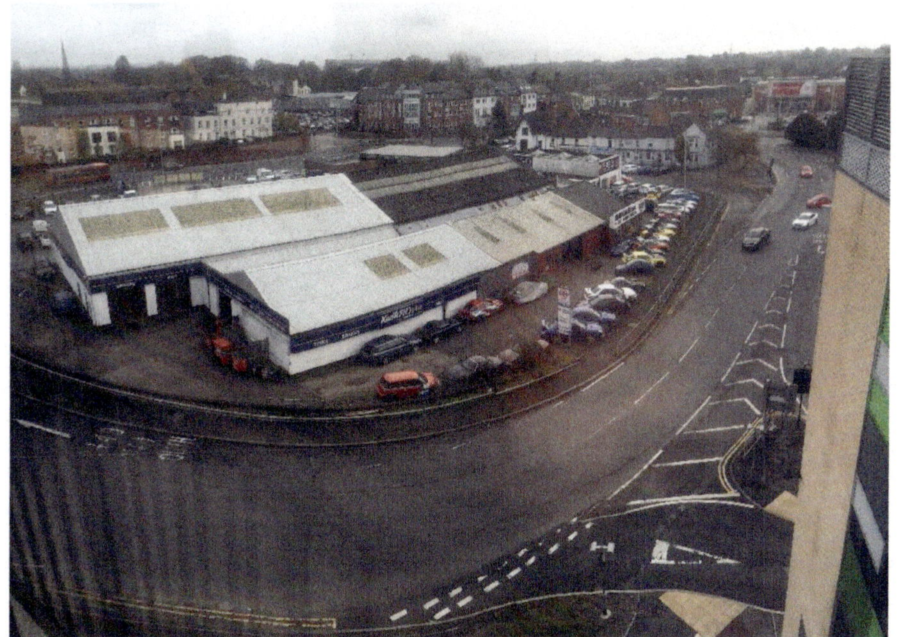

Sam Wane

Wedgwood Life

Life at Wedgwood:
waking up in front of the museum.
The beautiful sunrise,
the horizon:
waking up early to watch it.
Experience the lovely view:
ditch your homework,
to see the Wedgwood blue.
Living the Wedgwood life.

Walk around:
you smell the English breakfast.
The dining hall,
the tearoom:
with scones and cakes,
the scents of paint:
lunar being decorated.
Living the Wedgwood life.

The birds:

waking up to the songs they sing.

Attempting to sing with them:

failing miserably.

The laughter:

children on their bikes,

playing in back gardens.

Living the Wedgwood life.

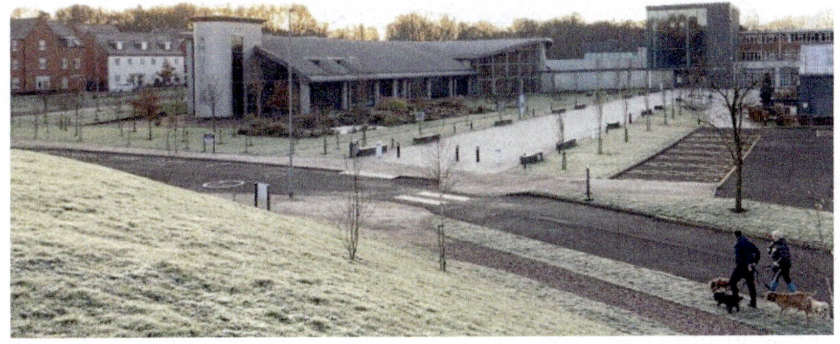

Lydia Kaufman

Where John Donne Gone?

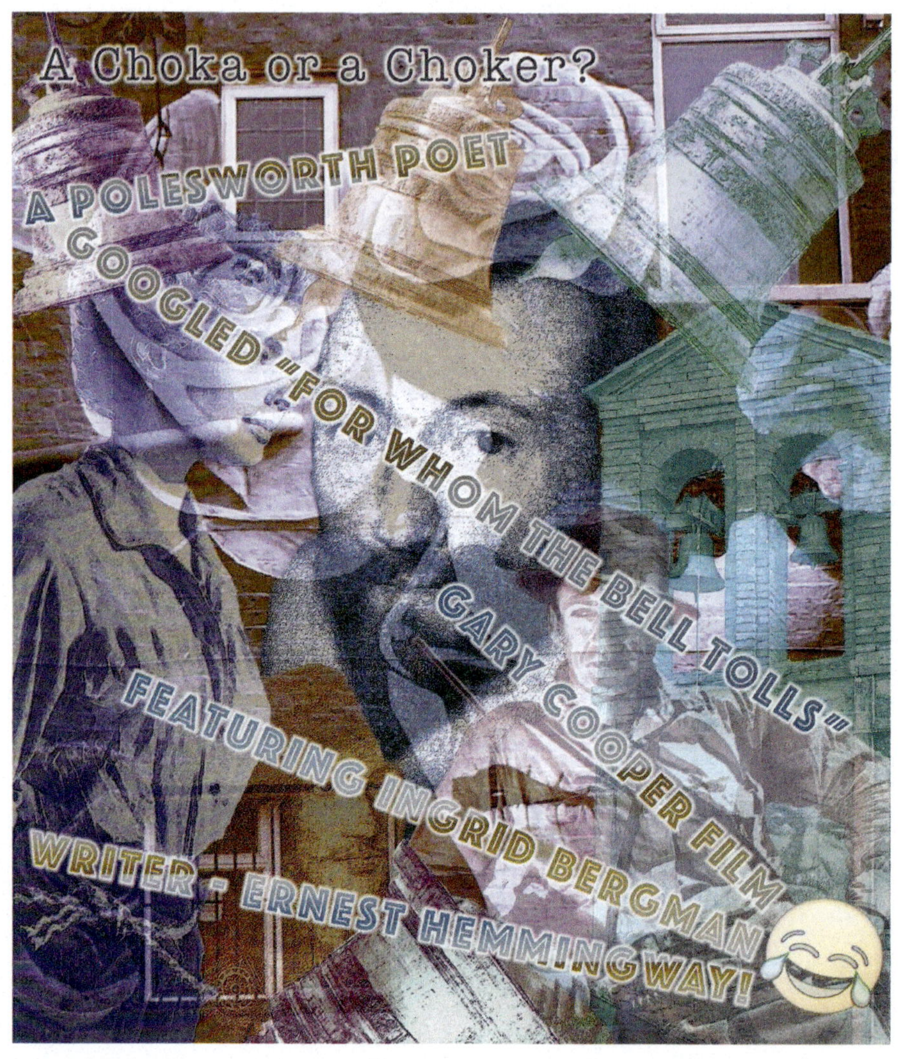

John Carpenter

ABOUT KATHARINE HOUSE HOSPICE

‘Katharine House Hospice aim is to enable our patients with life limiting condition and those close to them to live life as fully as possible and make the most of the time that they have.

Our care is free and provided where and when it is needed most: at the hospice, in the community and at home.

Katharine House Hospice began as ‘Stafford Hospice at Home’ in 1989, before the Katharine House Hospice Day Care Unit opened in May 1993. We have gone from strength to strength, welcoming our first in-patient in September 2000, a ‘Drop in Day’ in 2001 and a Carers’ Group in 2004.

Today’s Katharine House Hospice continues to grow, with over 200 staff and a staggering 600+ volunteers. Together we provide care for the families of mid-Staffordshire and we could not have done this without the support of our local community.

All of our services are offered free of charge. As a charity we rely on the kindness and generosity of the local community to help generate 2/3rds of the funds needed (approx. £3m each year) to continue our care.

Our Caldicott Guardians are Neil Grannon, Director of Care and Dr. Stala Polyviou

Here at Katharine House Hospice, our aim is to enable our patients and those close to them to live life as fully as possible and make the most of the time that they have. We offer a welcoming, warm and safe environment, where hope is kept alive and laughter is often heard.

We provide a range of services which offer holistic care and support for people with advanced life-limited conditions across mid-Staffordshire.

Many people believe that we treat cancer patients only, however we care for people with a range of conditions including Multiple Sclerosis, Motor Neurone Disease, end-stage Renal failure and cancer.

From our Day Therapies Unit, our 10-bed In-Patient Unit, the Wellbeing Day programme to care "At Home", carer support and the Lymphoedema Clinic, our aim is to enable patients to live their lives as fully and as comfortably as possible whilst providing support to their families/carers.

All of our services are offered free of charge. We are a charity and we rely on the kindness and generosity of the local community to help generate 2/3rds of the funds needed (almost £3m each year) to continue our care.'

(https://www.khhospice.org.uk/your-hospice/) (ACCESSED 1/8/22)

ABOUT WORD STAFFORD

WORD is a regular event combining a poetry slam, open mic and spoken word performance. Usually held at venues in the county town of Stafford, WORD Stafford is Stafford's only regular spoken word event, and additionally involves online events, videos, and competitions to enter.

WORD Stafford is organised by Mel Wardle Woodend and Blind Johnny Smoke.

Find out more about WORD Stafford at

https://www.facebook.com/WORDstafford/

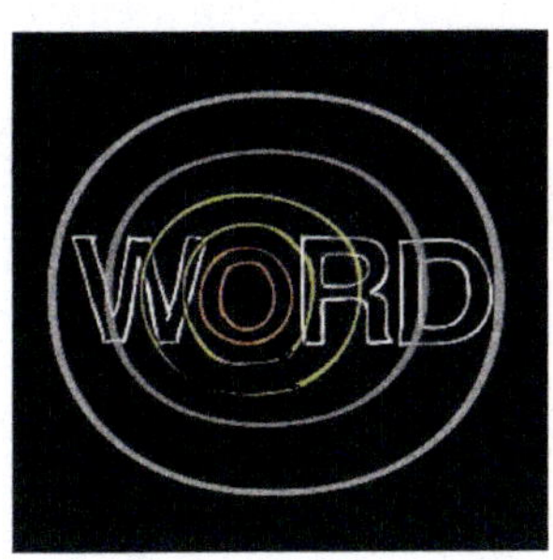

DREAM WELL WRITING LTD

Dream Well Writing Ltd are Staffordshire based publishers of dyslexia friendly books – with worldwide distribution and an environmentally conscious ethos – founded in 2017 by Mel Wardle Woodend Staffordshire Poet Laureate 2019 – 2022.

Find out more about Dream Well at

http://dreamwellwriting.simplesite.com/

https://www.facebook.com/dreamwellwriting/

dreamwellwriting@gmail.com

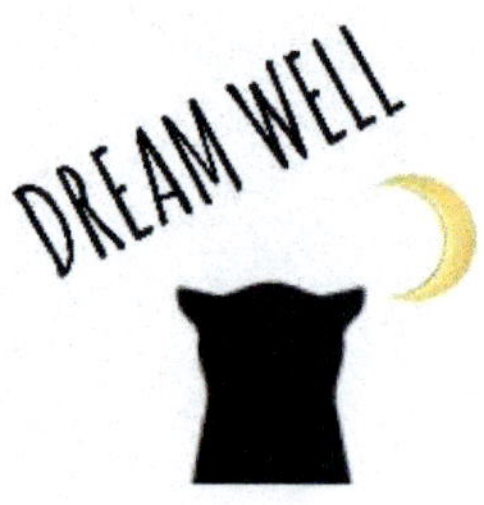

ALL MONIES FROM THE SALES OF THIS BOOK

(AFTER PRINTING COSTS)

WILL BE DONATED TO KATHARINE HOUSE HOSPICE

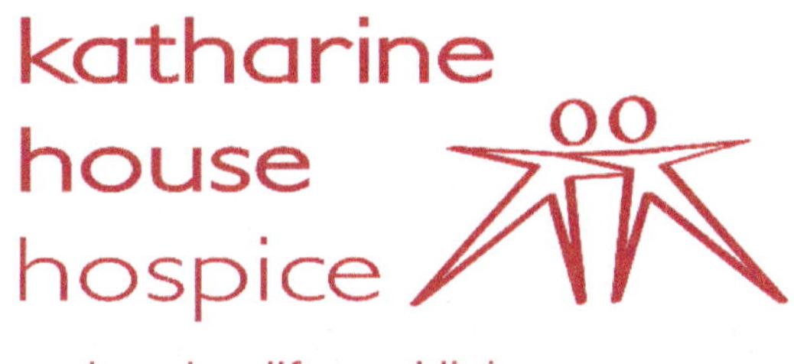

THANK YOU FOR YOUR SUPPORT

Printed in Great Britain
by Amazon